1964

Our Debt to Greece and Rome

EDITORS

GEORGE DEPUE HADZSITS, PH.D.

DAVID MOORE ROBINSON, PH.D., LL.D.

ARISTOPHANES
HIS PLAYS AND HIS INFLUENCE

BY
LOUIS E. LORD

COOPER SQUARE PUBLISHERS, INC.
NEW YORK
1963

Published 1963 by Cooper Square Publishers, Inc.

59 Fourth Avenue, New York 3, N. Y.

Library of Congress Catalog Card No. 63-10302

To

MY MOTHER

αἱ Χάριτες τέμενός τι λαβεῖν ὅπερ οὐχὶ πεσεῖται
ζητοῦσαι, ψυχὴν εὗρον Ἀριστοφάνους

PLATO TO ARISTOPHANES

Striving to win for herself a shrine to endure everlasting,
Poesy searching long found Aristophanes' soul

PREFACE

IN this little volume I have tried to give some account of Aristophanes' plays and his influence. In a book intended for readers not familiar with the conventions of the ancient drama it has seemed worth while to include a brief account of the origin of Greek comedy and a description of the Greek theater.

I have discussed Aristophanes' influence in Germany, France and England only, with a few incidental references to Spain and Italy. Even in this limited sphere it has been possible (and probably desirable) to mention only the more notable instances of Aristophanes' influence.

Constant use has been made of the recent German monographs on Aristophanes mentioned in the bibliography, especially Süss' valuable work. The quotations from Aristophanes are from the translation by Mr. B. B. Rogers. For permission to quote this translation I am deeply indebted to the publishers,

Messrs. George Bell and Sons. Mr. Rogers
has edited each play with a charming introduction, a translation and notes at once
scholarly and interesting. I can not too highly
commend this translation to those who do not
know Aristophanes in the Greek, and the notes
and introductions to those who do. It is such
a commentary as Aristophanes himself would
enjoy.

To my colleague, Professor Albert W. Aron,
I am indebted for many helpful suggestions
and for that final test of friendly courtesy —
an offer to read my proofs. I should like also
to record my indebtedness to my friend, Professor Charles B. Martin, under whose sympa-
thetic interpretation I made my first joyous
acquaintance with Aristophanes. To my wife's
keen and kindly criticism is due whatever
merit this book may be judged to possess, and
I may perhaps be allowed to express here the
inadequacy of this acknowledgment in the
words of the Sicilian, ἦ μεγάλα χάρις δώρῳ
σὺν ὀλίγῳ.

CONTENTS

[xi]

ARISTOPHANES
HIS PLAYS AND HIS INFLUENCE

ARISTOPHANES

HIS PLAYS AND HIS INFLUENCE

I. THE ORIGIN OF GREEK COMEDY
— THE GREEK THEATER

SHELLEY in the Preface to his *Hellas* says: "We are all Greeks. Our laws, our literature, our religion, our arts have their roots in Greece. But for Greece — Rome the instructor, the conqueror, or the metropolis of our ancestors, would have spread no illumination with her arms and we might still have been savages and idolaters." Even the most ardent supporters of the classical tradition today might be inclined to modify this statement; but of both tragedy and comedy it is emphatically true. In its essentials the modern drama is derived from the Greeks of Athens. An independent drama may have developed elsewhere but the English drama not only had its origin in Greece but the Greeks developed both tragedy and comedy to such perfection that in two thousand years little has been added to their achievements except in the production of scenic effects.

Of the origin of tragedy it is not the purpose of this work to speak. Its beginnings are fairly clear. Of comedy the same cannot be said. Even the great Aristotle was somewhat in doubt. "The successive changes through which Tragedy passed and the authors of these changes are well known, whereas Comedy has had no history because it was not at first treated seriously. It was late before the Archon granted a comic chorus to a poet; the performers were till then voluntary. Comedy had already taken definite shape when comic poets, distinctively so called, are heard of. Who introduced masks or prologues, or increased the number of actors . . . these and other similar details remain unknown. As for the plot, it came originally from Sicily; but of Athenian writers Crates was the first who, abandoning the 'iambic' or lampooning form, generalized his themes and plots."[1] Surprisingly little can be added to what Aristotle has said.

The Greek comedy arose from two sources: first from the so-called 'comos' or song of revelry. These songs frequently combined two elements, charms or incantations to avert evil and prayers for the blessing of fertility. Such songs were sung by bands of revelers on various occasions, but those from which comedy developed were sung in honor of the god of wine, Dionysus. There were two festivals in honor of this god at Athens: the *Lenaea* near the end of January and the *City* or *Great Dionysia* celebrated toward the end of March. At these festivals bands of revelers, often dressed in ludicrous costumes, sang chants interspersed with rude ribaldry in honor of the god. They carried with them elevated on a pole the phallic symbol and the burden of their songs was a prayer for fertility. Such choruses sometimes paraded through the villages singing uncomplimentary and excessively personal serenades. As these choruses were developed, responses were offered by the audience or by groups from the audience. These groups were gradually admitted into the chorus until it became a twofold body composed of elements which expressed their rivalry in antiphonal song. An example of such a chorus in the developed comedy may be seen in one of Aristophanes' plays where half the chorus

[5]

are city women and the other half women from the country. These songs were rude in character and very coarse in their nature, but the singers were the ministrants through whom the community worshiped its god of fertility. The invention of the comic chorus is sometimes attributed to Susarion.

So far the development of these choruses had little relation to the later Attic comedy; but now a second element was added which made the drama possible. In Sicily a rude mime or farce had been developed under the influence of two poets especially, Epicharmus and Sophron. These farces were intimately familiar and the jests were made almost exclusively at the expense of persons who were in the audience. In some way these Dorian farces (Sicily was largely a Doric community) were joined with these comic songs of Attica. The fact that both the Doric mime and the Attic 'comos' were much given to personalities made this union an easy and a compatible one. The personal allusions of the comos had been of a more or less haphazard nature — they were extemporized by the volunteers of whom Aristotle speaks. The personalities of the mime were woven into a more or less definite plot, requiring more preparation and doubtless producing a more satisfactory effect upon the unhappy victims. Improvisation was probably not excluded altogether. In this respect these early mimes suggest the *Comedia del' Arte*. A later development of the Doric mime may be seen in the recently discovered works of Herodas and the literary mimes included with the pastorals of Theocritus.

The inhabitants of the little town of Megara, a Doric eye-sore on the border of Attic soil, claim the credit of producing the first comedy. The virulent vigor with which the Athenians deny this claim leads the impartial reader to believe in its justice. The Athenians protest too much. However and wherever the union may have occurred the comedy of Athens was born of these two elements, the phallic songs of fertility and the Dorian mime, whose introduction made the plot possible.

For the predecessors of Aristophanes a word may suffice. They are known only through literary references and slight fragments. Magnes, as Aristophanes says, introduced choruses of birds, frogs, harp-players, and Lydians, but could not hold the favor of his audiences. Cratinus was the real founder of

Attic comedy. An appreciation of the rapid growth of Greek comedy and of Aristophanes' achievement can be reached when it is noticed that his activity was so near the beginning of the art that his *Clouds* was defeated by Cratinus' *Wine Flask*. Cratinus' first victory in comedy precedes Aristophanes' birth by only about five years. Crates, of whom Aristotle says in the passage quoted that he gave up the more personal and bitter type of satire and devoted himself to the portrayal of character, was a contemporary of Cratinus. Eupolis was a rival of Aristophanes, and these two together with Cratinus were chosen to represent the Old Attic Comedy in the Alexandrian canon.

The Greek theater is so different from the modern theater that it is worth while to notice the setting in which these comedies were produced.[2]

The Greek dramas were performed in an open air theater without roof. A hillside was selected whose slope, curving inward, offered a convenient place upon which an audience could sit and watch the performance in the space below. Later, as the cities increased in wealth, these natural theaters were partially excavated, the sides were extended and supported by masonry, seats of stone, or even marble, were added. The seats were divided into wedges by aisles that converged toward the bottom, and the lower seats were separated from the upper by a broad aisle running around the theater transversely. Above this the number of converging aisles was doubled. Below, on the level ground, in the space enclosed by the seats and the stage building was a complete circle, in the larger theaters some sixty feet in diameter. This circle was called the 'orchestra' or dancing place. Its circumference was marked by a ring of stones set flush with the ground. Generally in the center though sometimes at the side or in front was an altar to the god Dionysus in whose honor the plays were presented.

Back of the orchestra was a narrow space on which the actors performed their parts. Whether or not this space was raised as is the modern stage is still a moot question. In any case it was not raised for a long time to any great elevation and access to it from the orchestra was easy. The chorus occupied the orchestra from the time of their entrance to the close of the play. There they performed their dances about the altar of Dionysus and thence they and their leader conversed with the actors. They might even leave the orchestra and join the actors on the 'stage' if the economy of the play demanded. Back of the 'stage' was the front of the scene-building (the modern scene), adorned with pillars and pierced with three doors leading to the dressing rooms behind.

In tragedy this background most commonly represented a palace or temple to which the pillars belong. If a private house was represented, as in comedy, then the pillars may be conceived as part of a portico before the house.[3] Removable panels inserted between the pillars could be painted to suggest other scenes. Change of scene was infrequent. Little effort was made to secure realism in this scenery; attention was concentrated on the costumes, the incidental music, graceful or provocative dancing and clever acting.

In the earlier plays the action occurs in a great variety of places but as the comedy developed the scene is more and more frequently laid on an Athenian street. So established did this convention become that Plautus prides himself on his veracity in admitting that the

Menaechmi is a Sicilian play and not falsely claiming, as do his rivals, that all his plots are laid in Athens.

The fact that the action takes place on a street or at least in the open air robs the Greek and Latin plays of much of the 'business' which is so large a part of the production of a modern comedy. Consider what Mr. Shaw's plays would be without the stage directions. Anyone who has seen the revival of a Latin Comedy must have noticed that events seldom occur — they are merely talked about.

These Greek theaters, as their ruins show today, had wonderful acoustic properties. So satisfactory are they that an actor with a good voice, aided by the scene-building which served as a sounding board, could be easily heard by an audience of fifteen or twenty thousand. In all plays, both tragedy and comedy, the actors wore masks. Thus the free play of facial expression which gives the modern actor his opportunity for the portrayal of emotion was lost. But in an audience so large as that which frequently witnessed a Greek play only a small number, comparatively, could be near enough to catch the play of feature on the actor's face. It may, however, be said that there is little room for choice between an ancient mask of painted cloth and a modern mask of painted and powdered skin. Further it is by no means certain that the tragic or comic mask was an inartistic device. Mr. Gordon Craig says that "the mask is the only right medium for portraying the expression of the soul as shown through the expression of the face . . . they will be used in place of the human face in the near future." [4]

Access to the stage and the orchestra was obtained not only through the scene-building but by a wide passage at either side which ran between the theater proper and the scene-building. These passages (*parodoi*) were regularly used by the chorus.

It has often been remarked that the Greeks chose for their temples sites of commanding beauty, and the same thing may be affirmed with equal truth of their theaters. A drama must have had compelling interest that could draw the attention even of one familiar with the landscape from the fair panorama beyond the scene-building and confine his gaze to the stage. If the interest flagged the Athenian could raise his eyes from the orchestra and the chorus and look out across the lovely plain to where Hymettus lifts its thyme-covered slopes. He could see the long walls running toward Phaleron, and if his seat were high enough he could catch a glimpse of the blue gulf, and beyond, Aegina in the haze. Or if the play were at Delphi, below the spectator lay Apollo's mighty temple and his awesome shrine, toward which ran the sacred way with all its memorials of the victory of Greek over barbarian and of Greek over Greek. He could see the gloomy rock whence flows the Castalian spring and, a sheer thousand feet below, the deep gorge with its olive groves and the white winding way down which Oedipus strode so hastily in his fruitless effort to avoid Apollo's doom.

Competition alike in athletics and art seemed to the Greek the most natural way in which to stimulate and to test achievement. Hence the development of the great athletic contests with their attendant competitions in music and oratory. So it was quite in keeping with Greek practice that at Athens plays were always presented in competition with each other and a prize was awarded to the victor.

Since the production of a play involved much expense for the costumes and for training the actors, and since the leisure time of even an Athenian citizen was limited, only three comedies were presented at each of the great Athenian festivals. The official in charge of these performances (the archon) selected from the plays offered the three most promising in his opinion and to each he "granted a chorus." That is, he authorized their production in the competition. Judges selected by lot from the audience ranked the three plays in the order of their excellence. To be awarded third place was, therefore, to be placed among those who "also ran."

The structure of an Attic Comedy is unlike anything at present known on the stage. The play regularly began with a scene between two or three actors. In the course of their dialogue the setting for the drama was disclosed to the audience. This scene in its essence was much like the opening of any modern play. At the close of this scene the chorus appeared singing its entrance song (the *parodos*). The chorus consisted of twenty-four men who were dressed often in the most fantastic manner. Sometimes they represented men riding on ostriches or dolphins, sometimes huge wasps, or frogs, or clouds, or birds. The effects thus produced must often have been very ridiculous, sometimes very beautiful. The chorus might be divided into two semi-choruses, representing different factions in the audience. Each half-chorus had its own leader and the leader of one of these semi-choruses acted as the leader of the entire group when they were united. After the close of the entrance song the chorus remained in the orchestra before the spectators until the end of the play. There followed a scene which is characteristic of every comedy. This is the so-called *agon* or contest. In this two rival actors contend for opposite principles, it may be for the old or the new education, for the old or new type of poetry, for a government of the state by women. This contest always closed with a victory on the part of one of the actors. The other acknowledged himself vanquished or his defeat was decreed by another actor or by the chorus. The actors then withdrew from the stage. The chorus faced the audience and advancing toward them sang its great song, the *parabasis*.

This is a unique feature of Attic Comedy. In it the poet speaks through the mouth of his chorus. He declares his preferences in lit-

erature and in statecraft. He is often personal. He does not hesitate to refer by name
to people in the audience and he covers with
the most scathing scorn all those who are his
political enemies or artistic rivals. In its complete development the *parabasis* is a very elaborate composition consisting of nine parts,
each carefully arranged and conforming to
rules quite as arbitrary as those which govern
the sonnet. In some of the *parabases* all of
the nine parts do not appear and as the comedy developed there was a tendency to sup-
press this feature of the play.

As the strains of the *parabasis* died away
the actors appeared again. Several short
scenes followed, separated by choral songs.
In these scenes the policy adopted as a result
of the 'contest' was applied to concrete cases.
For instance, in the *Women in Parliament* it
is decided that the state will best be served by
turning the government over to the women.
The latter part of the play shows how excel-
lently the women govern in different exigen-
cies. After a number of these episodes have
demonstrated the benefits or the ridiculous
catastrophes that follow the adoption of the
approved policy the actors withdraw and the

chorus sings its final song as it withdraws in wild revelry.

This may be regarded as the typical structure of a comedy; but the plays of Aristophanes show a great many variations from it. The 'contest' may follow the *parabasis* as in the *Frogs*. There may be two contests, as in the *Knights* and the *Clouds*. The final song and dance of the chorus may be lacking, as in the *Knights*. There may be two *parabases* as in the *Clouds* and the *Birds;* or there may be none as in the *Women in Parliament* and the *Plutus*. The poet was still master of his art, he had not yet become its servant — the rules were made for the poet, not the poet for the rules.

The first thing that a modern reader notices in an Attic Comedy is its lack of plot. In a few of the plays, as the *Women at the Festival of Demeter,* one consistent idea is followed and the play may be said to have a plot in the sense that a modern comedy has. In most of the extant comedies of Aristophanes, however, the poet is interested in showing how ridiculous or how advantageous it would be to follow a certain policy. This he does by many concrete illustrations of its application to individual instances, and to individuals. It is, par excellence, an *argumentum ad hominem*. In fact the unfortunate *homo* was often named and pointed out by the actor. There is very little of what we call 'business' in a Greek Comedy. It is, as has been said, a 'dramatized debate.'

Of all the modern types of plays the Attic Comedy most nearly resembles the light opera at its best. It has about it a corresponding gorgeousness of costume, the same beauty of setting, and it must be confessed a similar appeal to the lower passions. For the Greek Comedy is often broad and vulgar in the extreme. It has the same fondness for unreal and whimsical situations, a world turned topsy-turvy. It has the same tendency to minimize the plot and merely add scene to scene. It has the same buffoonery which often appears in the prose scenes of the light opera. The tramp and the clown who make their burlesque way across the comic opera stage are not too different from the slaves and the buffoon of the Attic Comedy. Beautiful music was quite as essential to a successful Greek Comedy as beautiful costumes and beautiful lines, and the catchy songs from a comedy were sung on the streets of Athens for many days after a successful performance.

The light opera and the Attic Comedy were alike used by the playwright to hit off in a ridiculous way the idiosyncrasies of well-known individuals. Indeed the freedom with which persons are attacked in a Greek Comedy is its most distinctive feature. Nothing like it has ever appeared in the world. When the leading poets and statesmen of the day went up to the theater either at the *Lenaea* in January, when the Athenians celebrated the vintage, or at the *Great Festival of Dionysus* in the spring, when foreign ambassadors were present, they might expect to see a comedy brought upon the stage in which they were the leading characters. Actors would appear wearing masks closely resembling their victims' faces, and their most cherished poems or their most beloved policies might be held up to the most unmerciful criticism. The modern political cartoon is no more partisan, no more exaggerated, no more vindictive. It is true that the individual was often regarded merely as a type, but that could hardly soothe the feelings of the individual. Cleon, smarting from Aristophanes' satire, attempted to be revenged by process of law. How keenly the poet's ridicule was felt, how far his influence reached, Socrates makes clear when, on trial for his life, he speaks of the prejudice caused by the misrepresentation of Aristophanes as the hardest thing against which he had to contend.

The analogy with the comic opera must not be pressed too far. There was a seriousness of purpose about the old comedy which the opera lacks, the personal and local elements were more prominent, but if an effect at all similar to the comedies of Aristophanes is to be sought in the modern drama the nearest approach to that effect is found in such operas as those of Gilbert and Sullivan.

II. THE ATHENS OF
ARISTOPHANES [5]

OF THE private life of Aristophanes little is known. He was born an Athenian citizen some time in the decade following 450 B.C. He was thus a contemporary of those great men who crowned the age of Pericles with glory and whose names are household words wherever western civilization has gone.

The Delian League had been organized at the close of the Persian Wars as a protection against the aggression of the Great King. The treasury of the League had been transferred in 454 B.C. from Delos to Athens and the growing power of the Athenian Commonwealth had gradually changed the position of Athens from that of a leading member of the League to that of Mistress of an Empire. Pericles had not hesitated to devote the funds of the League to the beautification of the imperial city. Jealousy at once flared up in the other cities. Distrust of Athenian rule, a sense of security from further Persian invasions and the consequent belief that the League was no longer necessary, all these together with the arrogant and haughty behavior of the Athenians were causes which contributed to a general dissatisfaction and finally brought about the revolt of the other states. Narrow-minded, unpatriotic Sparta, envious that Athens should have reaped so large a proportion of the benefits of the Persian wars, saw her chance to be revenged on her traditional rival. At the outbreak of the Peloponnesian War she placed herself at the head of the opposition to Athens and fostered revolt among her allies.

The Peloponnesian War is the most heartbreaking war in history. Again and again the historian can place his finger on an unimportant event and say: "If only this had been altered, the enlightened cause of Athens would have triumphed." The early death of Pericles, a brief delay in Sicily, the failure of the Athenians to prevent the Spartan general Gylippus and his escort from entering Syracuse, an eclipse of the moon, the banishment of Alcibiades, a chance storm at sea, criminal negligence at the Hellespont, each in its turn dashed victory from the hands of Athens.

The Peloponnesian War began in 431 B.C.

and dragged its weary course till 404 B.C.
Thus most of Aristophanes' productive life was
coincident with this war. When Aristophanes
produced his first play Athens was the all but
undisputed mistress of northern Greece and
the islands of the Aegean Sea. Her navies
came and went unchallenged from Egypt to
the Crimea, from Byzantium to Marseilles.
The imperial city's power was almost unlim-
ited. Less than fifty years before Aristophanes' birth the Athenians had won the great
victories of Marathon and Salamis. The long
walls that joined Athens to its ports, Phaleron
and the Piraeus, had been completed only ten
years when he was born. He lived to see his
city shorn of all her power, her fleets scattered
and dismantled, her commerce wrecked, her
people reduced to starvation, the olive orchards
cut down and the long walls which had been
the symbol of her greatness demolished to the
music of flutes. Aristophanes had been a
member of the first and most complete democracy the world has ever seen. He lived to see
this democracy succeeded by an oligarchy of
Four Hundred. He saw Alcibiades lead forth
to Sicily the most magnificent armament that
any Greek state ever put to sea. He witnessed

[23]

the relief expedition sent out to retrieve the blunders which the cautious Nicias made at the siege of Syracuse, and together with his countrymen he must have been stunned by the news of the entire annihilation of both these navies. He rejoiced with his friends in the victory of the Athenians at Arginusae and he was probably in the Assembly that morning when Socrates sturdily refused to allow the people to vote on the execution of the generals who won that victory, because such action was unconstitutional. He saw the government of the Four Hundred overturned by the willful and brilliant Alcibiades. He saw Alcibiades again swept into exile. He must have been in Athens that terrible night when the Sacred Trireme alone of all the Athenian navy came into the Piraeus with the news that the fleet had been captured in the Hellespont by the Spartans. The wailing cry that ran from the Piraeus up the long walls to the city must have aroused him too. He saw Lysander besiege Athens and he witnessed the final destruction of the city walls. He suffered the misrule of the Thirty Tyrants who were placed over the city by the Spartans. He fortunately lived to see the Thirty give way to the Ten and the

Ten to the restoration of the old constitution.
He saw the long walls rise again, this time
curiously enough with the aid of the very Persians whose defeat, one hundred years before,
the building of these walls had signalized. He
saw the power of Sparta wane and, the very
year after the second production of his final
play, the *Plutus,* in 387 B.C., he saw the Lord
of Persia impose the King's Peace on the free
Greek cities. His life began during the greatest period of Athenian history, it coincides with
her long decline during the Peloponnesian War
and ends just before the humiliation of Sparta
at the hands of Thebes, when Athens was
beginning to rise again and reëstablish her
leadership among the members of her old
confederacy.

It was a dramatic time of fluctuating standards and changing ideals. When Aristophanes
was born, the shining columns of the Parthenon which Ictinus and Callicrates reared, were
just beginning to rise on the south side of the
Acropolis. He saw the Erechtheum with its
graceful porches replace the shrine of a sim-
pler and cruder day. While Aristophanes was
still a lad Pericles began the stately Propylaea
which guards the entrance to Athena's Hill.

[25]

It was little wonder that the poet, who in his youth saw these buildings fashioned by the most skillful masons Europe has ever known, should have made his own the tribute of the Theban poet, Pindar: " Oh rich and renowned and with violets crowned, Oh Athens the envied of Nations." [6]

But this abundant blooming of the flower of Greek art had not taken place without a change in the morals of the people. Phidias was the sculptor of Aristophanes' youth. His majestic statues of the gods had lent an added dignity to the religious conceptions of his countrymen. They bespoke the august serenity of an earlier age. But even as the Parthenon drew to completion a change could be seen in the artistic spirit. As the worshiper approached the great east portal, before his eyes could rest on the resplendent statue of Athena within, his upward glance caught the work of the younger generation on the frieze above the door. There sat the gods at ease, not the ancient dwellers on Olympus, the seat of the gods that standeth fast for ever, not shaken by the winds or vext with rain,[7] but graceful and intimate beings taking their pleasure in quite mortal fashion. Grace and beauty were there, but not dignity or strength. The austere majesty of Phidias was to give way to the refined beauty of Praxiteles. It was not only philosophy which this generation was bringing down from heaven to dwell among men. The gods were fast becoming mortal.

The same tendencies were at work in the field of literature. When Aristophanes was born, Pindar's career was drawing to a close in despised Thebes. Aeschylus had died some ten years before, proud, if we may trust his epitaph, not of his tragedies but of his bravery against the Persians at Marathon and Salamis. The moral exaltation of Aeschylus and his "men who fought at Marathon" had given place to the clear serenity of Sophocles. When Aristophanes was born, Sophocles was at the height of his power. Only after many trials Euripides finally won his first dramatic victory. From that time till his death his many-sided genius, his warm humanity and his glittering rhetoric, his glorious lyrics and his sophisticated realism were strong factors in determining the literary taste of Athens. And during the twenty years that Aristophanes survived him, his relaxing influence gained in popularity. The judges of the theater may have awarded him a scanty number of prizes, but his songs were in the hearts of the people. When Aristophanes was born, Herodotus was still active. But, significantly enough, in 444 B.C. he was one of the colonists who went out to found Thurii in Italy.

In morals, education and religion, the deterioration from the old ideals was even more marked. Professors of rhetoric and professional speech writers were becoming a commonplace. A sophist who could defend with equal facility and brilliance either side of any question was no novelty. The ancient as well as the modern Greek was litigious, and the younger generation in the theater was beginning to prefer the rhetorical argumentation of Euripides' characters to the pellucid clearness of the Sophoclean narratives. The Greek speculative spirit was laying rough hands on sacred dogmas. Democritus was preaching the strange doctrine that the universe was but a collection of infinitely small bodies which he called atoms. The gods even were no longer safe, for Euripides had revealed their frailties. Scepticism on every subject was rife.

In education the required course of the good old days was being replaced by a disturbing elective system. Pertness in youth was not only common but commended. The jazz jaundice had attacked music and was casting a pale and sickly hue over the countenance of the good old battle hymns. Socrates — the chief of the sophists according to Aristophanes — had laid hold of philosophy and had dragged her from heaven to earth to answer such obvious questions as "What is justice?", "What is beauty?", or such pointless trifles as how many of his own feet a flea could leap or which end of the gnat produced the buzz. "By their fruits ye shall know them," but "What," may very well have been inquired, "is the fruit of these confusing and useless questions Socrates is always asking his fellow citizens? Have his pupils been better citizens for their association with him? Who are they? Critias, one of the Thirty Tyrants, and one of the worst of them; Alcibiades, with the intellect of a god and the judgment of a buffoon, who has done more than any single man to ruin his country; the rich Crito who has eschewed political life and the service of the state; Xenophon, the lover of Sparta, who has actually fought against his own city and has died in exile; Plato, the rank communist, with his seductive style beguiling as the voice of the Sirens." It is easy to say that Aristophanes' view of Socrates was distorted. True enough. But that Socrates' teaching was subversive of the accepted ideals in religion and conduct no man can deny. That he taught youths to regard gods whom the city did not regard is equally true, that he broke with convention is quite clear. On all these counts Aristophanes would have opposed him. For, " Aristophanes, an aristocrat by party allegiance, was from the beginning in opposition to democracy and progress, to the elevation of the masses, to the career open to talent, to free thought, to finer art, to art for art's sake, to community of goods, to women's rights, to every form of sophistic phrase-making and humanitarian claptrap." [8]

It is perhaps inevitable that a comedian should be a conservative. He must seize upon those aspects of society or upon those individuals who deviate enough from the normal to make them appear queer. Radicalism and reformers are always fair game for the writers of comedy or satire or for the comic press. A reference to the files of any comic journal will show that conservatism is a mild word to apply to their interest in any reform.

It was, then, in such an age that Aristophanes lived. The Age of Heroes was passed and the Age of Iron was come. In more senses than one the *Götterdämmerung*, the Twilight of the Gods, was descending on Athens.

III. ARISTOPHANES' PLAYS

THE first three plays that Aristophanes wrote were not brought out in his own name. They were produced in the name of the contemporary actors, but it is probable that the name of the real author was well known. The *Banqueters* appeared in 427 B.C. and the *Babylonians* in 426 B.C. The former was an attack on the new education and the latter an attack on the home and foreign policies of the Athenian state. Both of these plays have perished except for small fragments. The *Acharnians,* 425 B.C., which won first place, is still extant.

The most engrossing subject that could occupy the attention of the Athenians at this time, six years after the beginning of the Peloponnesian War, was the hardships that they were enduring from the overcrowding of the city and the destruction of the crops each summer. The great plague had decimated the city. Pericles, its ablest statesman, had succumbed to the disease. The people were eager for

peace but the assembly, under the domina-
tion of Cleon, still declared for war. The
folly of the war party is the subject of the
Acharnians.

The opening scene takes place in the Assembly where the stupidity and the gullibility
of the crowd are held up to ridicule. Dicaeopolis, a typical Athenian citizen, chafes at the
foolish waste of money on foreign embassies
and at the futility of his countrymen. Decid-
ing in disgust to make peace for himself, he
sends a private messenger to Sparta, who returns with samples of truces for five, for ten
and for thirty years. The Chorus enter, pur-
suing the messenger, and find Dicaeopolis
celebrating the festival of Dionysus. They
denounce him as a traitor and threaten to
stone him. They are about to put their
threat into execution when he seizes a charcoal hamper and a sword (the Chorus are
charcoal burners of Acharnae) and threatens
to destroy charcoal and hamper if they do not
give him a chance for his life. This scene is
a parody of the *Telephus* of Euripides where
the murder of the child Orestes is threatened.
Many of the lines are echoes of Euripides.
Since Dicaeopolis is to plead for his life, he

must present a pitiable spectacle, like a defendant before a jury. He therefore goes to the home of Euripides to beg for some of his tragic makeups. (For Euripides no longer represents the heroes of tragedy as demigods; they are at best uncompromised mortals and at the worst beggars appealing to the pity of the audience by their condition.) Euripides' servant greets Dicaeopolis in true Euripidean fashion. "My master is within and not within." "What do you mean?" says Dicaeopolis. "His mind is outside culling versicles but he himself is in the attic writing tragedies." Euripides is finally induced to lend Dicaeopolis the rags of Telephus, the Mysian, the most pitiable of his heroes. Then one after another the rest of a beggar's accessories are demanded till Euripides angrily protests: "Man, you're taking my whole tragedy." Arrayed in these rags, Dicaeopolis presents his case. Here follows a really bold argument against the continuance of the war. Lamachus, the leading general of the day, is called by the Chorus to support the opposite side. Of course Dicaeopolis is victorious in this banter of words, and the contest ends with him master of the situation.

In the *parabasis* that follows, Aristophanes explains how the state is indebted to him for his poetry and his wise counsel:

Let honor and praise be the guerdon, he says, of
* the poet whose satire has stayed you*
From believing the orators' novel conceits where-
* with they cajoled and betrayed you;*
Who bids you despise adulation and lies nor be
* citizens Vacant and Vain.*
For before, when an embassy came from the states
* intriguing your favor to gain,*
And called you the town of the VIOLET CROWN, *so*
* grand and exalted ye grew,*
That at once on your tiptails erect ye would sit,
* those* CROWNS *were so pleasant to you.*
And then if they added the SHINY, *they got what-*
* ever they asked for their praises,*
Though apter, I ween, for the oily sardine than for
* you and your city the phrase is.*
By this he's a true benefactor to you, and by show-
* ing with humor dramatic*
The way that our wise democratic allies are ruled
* by our state democratic.* (Vs. 633–642)

The latter part of the play is a broad farce carried to the point of indecency. It shows Dicaeopolis enjoying the benefits of his private peace. A Megarian enters chattering

barbaric Doric and sells his children disguised
as pigs. A Boeotian, also speaking in dialect
and displaying the stupidity which the clever
Athenians attributed to their northern neigh-
bors, sells Dicaeopolis eels from Lake Copais
and receives in return a thing which is common
in Athens and scarce in Thebes — namely an
Informer. Lamachus appears and is refused
access by Dicaeopolis to his private market.
Both then leave the stage to return again after
a short song by the Chorus, Lamachus severely
wounded, curiously enough under circum-
stances which later actually occurred. The
play closes with an uproarious scene which undoubtedly may be taken as reminiscent of the
early songs from which the comedy developed.

In the *Acharnians* Aristophanes had indi-
cated his intention to attack the demagogue
Cleon. This he did next year when at the
Lenaea (424 B.C.) he brought out the *Knights*.
To the casual reader, this play is one of the
least interesting of Aristophanes' dramas. It
is entirely political in its object. There are
but five characters and little action. In order
to appreciate it one must understand the political situation of the time. With the death
of Pericles the Assembly had fallen under the

sway of Cleon. It is difficult to estimate correctly this man's character for he is known chiefly through the caricature of Aristophanes and the *History* of Thucydides. Even this most impartial historian, when he speaks of Cleon, loses for a moment his remarkable aloofness and reserve. Cleon had been put in charge of the expedition against the Spartans at Sphacteria and had promised that he would bring the expedition to a successful conclusion within twenty days. "Then," says Thucydides, "the wiser sort of men were pleased when they reflected that of two good things they could not fail to obtain one, either it would be the end of Cleon, which they would have greatly preferred, or, if they were disappointed, he would put the Spartans into their hands." [9] Appearing in history in this plight it is hard for Cleon to obtain justice. In the plays of Aristophanes, he is certainly a demagogue, pure and unrelieved. Aristophanes attacked Cleon, as he himself boasts, "at the height of his power," for the *Knights* was produced only a short time after Cleon returned successful from the expedition to Sphacteria. For this he had been given a golden crown and the privilege of sitting in a place of honor at all public festivals. On the first occasion when he exercised this privilege he witnessed this play.

Aristophanes does not mention Cleon by name nor did the actor who took the leading part wear a mask resembling Cleon (it is said no actor dared to); but the audience, as Aristophanes himself says, were clever enough to see that the Paphlagonian tanner in the leading rôle was the same Cleon who was persuading them to follow his policies in the Assembly.

The characters of the play are Cleon, or the Paphlagonian, Demos (the Athenian People), a gullible old man, his two slaves, Nicias and Demosthenes (the leading generals of the day), who are jealous of the Paphlagonian's influence over Demos their master, and finally the Sausage-seller. The Chorus consists of the Knights who were hated by Cleon because they had forced him to disgorge a bribe of some five thousand dollars he had taken from the subject states.

An oracle has been discovered which is to rid the state of the Paphlagonian and liberate Demos from his influence. According to the oracle, the Paphlagonian is to be displaced by a Sausage-seller. This is none other than the

notorious Hyperbolus who did actually succeed Cleon as master of the Assembly.

The first half of the play consists of little
more than an exchange of coarse epithets and
jibes between the Sausage-seller and the
Paphlagonian. In the *parabasis* which follows
Aristophanes says that "Comedy Chorus in-
struction is quite the most difficult thing in
creation," as proved by the fate of the other
writers of Attic Comedy. The Chorus goes on
to relate the brave deeds of the Knights in the
recent expedition against Corinth.

Following the *parabasis*, the contest continues. The Sausage-seller out-Herods Herod
in his efforts to debauch Demos and win his
favor by sycophantic service. Incidentally
the characters of Nicias and Demosthenes are
well distinguished, the former, timid, pious,
superstitious, the latter, a bit given to spiritu-
ous liquor but downright, straightforward, sol-
dierly. A second *parabasis* contains a curious
discussion among the Ships of the fleet who
are unwilling to serve under Hyperbolus. At
the close of the play Demos is liberated from
the dominion of these wretched slaves and
brought back to the pristine glory which was
his in the good old days of Aristides and

Themistocles when the Persians were beaten
at Marathon and Salamis.

The next year (423 B.C.) Aristophanes presented the *Clouds*, but was unsuccessful, re-
ceiving only third place. He later revised the
play and it is the second edition which has
survived. It is an attack on the new education,
a subject already treated in the *Banqueters*.

new education

The chief character in the play is Socrates
and for this reason the play has always possessed great interest. The Socrates of the play
is a travesty on the real Socrates. Browning
makes Aristophanes say in his *Apology:*

> Socrates? No, but that pernicious seed
> Of sophistry whereby hopeful youth is taught
> To jabber argument, chop logic, pore
> On sun and moon, and worship Whirligig.

But the Athenian crowd were not keen to dis-
tinguish between the caricature and the reality.
And so effective was the satire that in the
minds of many the caricature actually replaced
the reality. Twenty years later when Socrates
was brought to trial on a capital charge he felt
constrained to say (if Plato is to be trusted)
that it was more difficult for him to dispel the
popular misconception of his teachings created

by this play than to answer the formal charge preferred by his accusers. He describes the accusations made by Aristophanes with such detail and pleads so earnestly for a fair hearing, unbiased by memories of that ludicrous portrait, that it is impossible to escape the conclusion that this play was one of the chief causes for his conviction and execution. It is a vivid proof of the potent influence of Aristophanes, for better or worse, on his own generation. The question of the relation existing between these two men was to be the subject of acrimonious dispute occupying the attention of German scholars for more than a century.

Strepsiades has been driven to distraction by the fast life that his son Pheidippides is leading and by the debts that he has incurred. Pheidippides' devotion to horse racing has ruined him and his only escape from paying his debts will be to have his son learn the new education. For one who is initiated into the school of the sophists, who make the worse appear the better reason, can persuade a jury that black is white. Thus Strepsiades can escape the payment of his debts. The son flatly refuses. He has no intention of joining those

lean philosophers and so losing his complexion.
The old man himself, therefore, goes to Socrates' " Thinking Shop " to learn his magic.
Socrates is disclosed swinging aloft in a basket
" treading on air and looking down on the
sun." The pupils are taught many curious devices and unusual lessons, the composition of
the universe, likewise all the mysteries beneath
the earth, and the fact that Zeus is no longer
king but that a Whirl has taken his place on
Olympus. Strepsiades with a good deal of
dismay surrenders himself to Socrates and is
taken within to begin his career as a neophyte.
Socrates invokes the help of the Clouds in this
task:

*Come forth, come forth, dread Clouds, and to earth
    your glorious majesty show;*
*Whether lightly ye rest on the time-honored crest
    of Olympus environed in snow,*
*Or tread the soft dance 'mid the stately expanse of
    Ocean, the nymphs to beguile,*
*Or stoop to enfold with your pitchers of gold, the
    mystical waves of the Nile,*
*Or around the white foam of Maeotis ye roam, or
    Mimas all wintry and bare,*
*O hear while we pray, and turn not away, from the
    rites which your servants prepare.*

Socrates explains to Strepsiades the nature of the Clouds and Strepsiades in each case accurately misses the point of the explanation. The *Parabasis* which follows is from the second edition of the play. In it Aristophanes complains that the first edition was not appreciated. He soundly belabors the audience and the judges for their lack of discernment.

After the *Parabasis* Strepsiades is disclosed in the " Thinking Shop " wrapped up in a blanket on a couch. He is trying to devote himself to philosophical speculation but is hindered by the bedbugs which torment him. Socrates tests him with some simple questions but finds him utterly stupid. In regard to poetry, Strepsiades, asked which measure he prefers, says that in his opinion nothing equals the bushel. Socrates, disgusted, dismisses him and Strepsiades in despair forces his son Pheidippides to come and be taught in his stead. To Pheidippides appear two Arguments, the Just and the Unjust. The Just Argument upholds the old type of education in which the boys were trained in the good old days:

When Honour and Truth were in fashion with youth and Sobriety bloomed on our shore;

[43]

First of all the old rule was preserved in our school
that " boys should be seen and not heard;"
And then to the home of the Harpist would come
decorous in action and word
All the lads of one town, though the snow peppered
down, in spite of all wind and all weather;
And they sung an old song as they paced it along,
not shambling with thighs glued together;
" O the dread shout of War how it peals from
afar," or " Pallas the Stormer adore."
To some manly old air all simple and bare which
their fathers had chanted before,
And should any one dare the tune to impair and
with intricate twistings to fill,
Such as Phrynis is fain, and his long-winded train,
perversely to quaver and trill,
Many stripes would he feel in return for his zeal,
as to genuine music a foe.

The Unjust Argument promises the learner
that he will be freed from all of these re-
straints. He will be able to speak up smartly
and pertly, no tradition will hamper him.
Naturally it is this education that Pheidippides chooses, and the play closes with a series
of scenes in which the benefits of the new education are displayed. One creditor is refused
his principal and interest because he calls both

a cock and a hen a fowl, where one should be called a fowler and the other a fowless. A second is bidden to go hang because he expects his principal to accumulate interest and grow larger, though he cannot explain why the sea is no larger with all the rivers running into it. Everything is quite satisfactory until Pheidippides proposes to show his father that it is right for a son to beat his sire. That this is natural can be seen from the way in which the younger chickens treat their elders and because an old man is for a second time a child. Strepsiades with difficulty accepts this but he quite loses patience when Pheidippides proposes to show that it is also right for a son to beat his mother. Throwing the new education to the winds Strepsiades attacks the "Thinking Shop" of Socrates and sets it on fire. The play closes with a real climax, not the usual scene of boisterous revelry.

The next year in 422 B.C. Aristophanes won second place with the *Wasps*. This play is a satire on the Athenian judicial practice and especially on the fondness which many of the Athenians were manifesting for jury duty since the custom of paying the jury had come into vogue. The juries were large — five hundred

was not an unusual number — and many of
the Athenians spent their time in this civic
privilege. But more particularly Aristophanes
is ridiculing the way in which the demagogues,
especially Cleon, were using the law courts to
occupy the people and beguile them into thinking that they were really the power in the
state. Their haughty treatment of the subject states does not escape the poet's notice.

The leading part in the *Wasps* is given to
an old man who has gone crazy on the subject
of jury duty. His son has resorted to all sorts
of expedients to keep the old gentleman at
home. The door and the windows have been
securely barred, but the father climbs out the
chimney. Another method of escape attempted by the old gentleman is to cling beneath the belly of an ass — a parody on the
famous scene in the *Odyssey* where Odysseus
escapes from the Cyclops' cave by hanging
beneath a ram. The Chorus arrayed like
wasps take the old man's part but the son induces them to argue the matter. After a debate their consent is secured to a compromise,
the old man is to remain at home and judge a
suit between two dogs, Labes and Cyon (*i.e.*,
Laches and Cleon). This trial is naturally a

parody on Athenian judicial procedure. The character of the old man speedily breaks down, he goes from one mania to another and the play ends with a riotous scene, the old man dancing the indecent *cordax*.

There are two *parabases* in the *Wasps*, both occurring unusually near the close of the play. In the first Aristophanes complains of the slight put upon his *Clouds* by the judges and compliments himself for his bravery in attacking Cleon in the *Knights*. It is quite clear, however, that in the *Clouds* he had gone further in eliminating the element of indecency than an Attic audience would tolerate, and in the *Wasps* these obscenities again appear. Indeed it is perhaps possible to see from some inconsistencies in the plot of the *Wasps* just where these riotous scenes were added.

The *Peace* produced in 421 B.C., like the *Acharnians,* is an appeal to the people to come to some agreement with Sparta and end the war. In fact the so-called " Peace of Nicias " was ratified not long after this play was presented. Aristophanes' love for the extravagant and his whimsical fancy appear to good advantage in this play.

Trygaeus, a typical vine-growing Athenian,

wearied of the long war decides to seek assistance from Zeus. So mounted on a huge beetle, a parody of Euripides' Bellerophon on Pegasus, he soars up from Aetna to Heaven. Arriving there he finds that the gods in their disgust have abandoned the Greeks to War, who has imprisoned Peace in a dungeon and is preparing to pound the cities of Hellas to powder in a huge mortar. The Chorus composed of farmers who are not interested in the war now take part in freeing Peace. After Peace has been liberated Trygaeus descends to earth and marries one of her handmaids.

In the *parabasis* the poet again asserts his superiority over his rivals claiming that his plays are more wholesome and moral than theirs. The latter part of the play is devoted to scenes displaying the happy state to which those who can enjoy the blessings of peace may attain. This part of the play has much beauty of sentiment but it must be confessed that the action is not as interesting as in the other plays. Perhaps for this reason or because of the lack of broad and indecent burlesque this play received only second place. Throughout the play there appear those brilliant lyrics which make the author great as a poet as well

as a writer of comedy. The beauty of the
Attic landscape, the joy of the country life are
all here:

> O *to watch the grape of Lemnos*
> *Swelling out its purple skin,*
> *When the merry little warblings*
> *Of the Chirruper begin;*
> *For the Lemnian ripens early,*
> *And I watch the juicy fig*
> *Till at last I pick and eat it*
> *When it hangeth soft and big;*
> *And I bless the friendly seasons*
> *Which have made a fruit so prime,*
> *And I mix a pleasant mixture,*
> *Grating in a lot of thyme,*
> *— Growing fat and hearty*
> *In the genial summer time.* (Vs. 1159–1171)

Seven years elapsed between the *Peace*,
which appeared in 421 B.C., and the *Birds*, the
next play of Aristophanes which has survived.
Of all the comedies of Aristophanes this is perhaps the one which in modern times has been
most admired. In the beauty of its imagery,
its elusive charm, its whimsical conceits, it is
often compared to *A Midsummer Night's
Dream*. It won only second place. Two Athe-

nians, Peisthetaerus and Euelpides, dissatisfied
with the conditions of life at Athens, set forth
to discover or to found an ideal state. In the
guise of Peisthetaerus Alcibiades may possibly
be recognized. He has all of that young
gentleman's ambition, his unconventional ideas,
his lack of stability and his expansive opti-
mism. Euelpides on the other hand is a gullible
stupid, whose mistakes and misunderstandings
lend point and contrast to his companion's suggestions. In their search for this ideal state
they are guided by the Birds. The great
chorus is composed of twenty-four different
Attic birds.

Each actor in the chorus was dressed in the
plumage appropriate to the bird he represented and as the actors came on the stage
one at a time they must have produced a very
effective and beautiful picture. After the *parabasis* (which is one of the great poems of Greek
literature), the foundation of the " City of
Cloudcuckooborough " takes place. Different
types of Athenian citizens, the poet, the sooth-
sayer, the office seeker, the astrologer all apply
for admission and are rejected. When the city
is built, the Birds intercept all the incense
which rises from the sacrifices on earth, threat-

ening the gods with starvation. Prometheus comes down from heaven to reveal the plight of the gods and to encourage the builders. He appears on the stage shielded from the sight of all-beholding Zeus by an umbrella. Hungry and in despair the gods send envoys, Poseidon, Heracles, who is always a dull glutton in comedy, and Triballus, a barbarian god whom no one can understand. But the Birds demand the surrender of Hera, Zeus' own bride. To Poseidon this seems monstrous, but Heracles, whose appetite can no longer stand the strain, acquiesces readily with a reminiscence of the Trojan War, "What! shall we go to war for one woman? " A compromise is reached when Zeus agrees to surrender his daughter to Peisthetaerus and the play ends with the wedding festivities.

In 411 B.C. Aristophanes produced the *Lysistrata*. In this play as in the *Peace* and the *Acharnians* he makes a firm protest against the continuance of the Peloponnesian War. The peace of Nicias which was to have quieted Greece for fifty years was soon broken, and the *Lysistrata* was written when the war had been renewed and just after the terrible disaster which the Athenians experienced at Syracuse.

Though the poet scarcely mentions this defeat it is evidently uppermost in his mind and it must have been in the minds of all his hearers. The leading character of this play, Lysistrata, is a woman of bold genius who determines that the war shall be brought to an end whether the men will or no. She induces her fellow countrywomen to join her in her plot and women of Sparta undertake to persuade the women of their country to do likewise. One element of the humor of the play lies in the broad Doric which these women speak. It is very difficult to appreciate the fine points of this dialect which enriches the Greek language quite as much as the Scotch dialect does English literature. Many a turn which appealed to the humor of an Athenian audience inevitably escapes the modern reader. The women having laid their plans secede to the Acropolis and refuse to have intercourse with their husbands until peace is declared. The *Lysistrata* closes with a boisterous festival in the true Dionysiac style. There is much in the play to which a modern audience would object, but the keenness of its satire and the piquancy of its situations can not be denied. It is Aristophanes' first venture into the realm of the relations between men and women. Its success encouraged him to use a similar theme in two of his other extant plays.

The *Lysistrata* was performed in the fall. The following spring the *Thesmophoriazusae*, the "Women at the Festival of Demeter," was produced. Aristophanes is always witty but any mention of Euripides seems to have been an unfailing source of inspiration to him. His plays are filled with parodies of Euripides' tragic style and references to him are always of a satiric nature, but the *Thesmophoriazusae* is devoted entirely to ridicule of the poet. In several of his plays Euripides had presented women of unlovely character. Aristophanes is especially fond of referring to Phaedra as a typical Euripidean woman. And now the women in their festival, from which men are entirely excluded, debate the question of how they may best avenge themselves upon Euripides. Euripides hears of the impending disaster and determines to be represented at their meeting by an advocate. He first asked the tragic poet Agathon, whose effeminate appearance would make it easy to disguise him as a woman, to speak for him. Agathon flatly refuses but in the meantime some delicious parodies on Agathon's new-fangled style are offered:

All people be still;
Allow not a word from your lips to be heard,
For the Muses are here, and are making their odes,
In my Master's abodes.
Let Ether be lulled and forgetful to blow,
And the blue sea waves, let them cease to flow,
And be noiseless.
Sleep birds of the air with your pinions at ease;
Sleep, beasts of the field, with entranquillized feet;
Sleep, sleep and be still.

Euripides then appeals successfully to his kinsman, Mnesilochus. In a scene of boisterous merriment he sets forth, disguised as a woman, to champion Euripides. The Women's Assembly is in full cry. After listening to addresses by two of their number they are preparing to vote the death of Euripides when Mnesilochus comes forward and is allowed by the presiding officer to make a speech. Never has a speaker so disappointed his audience. Mnesilochus says, in effect, " Euripides did tell some strong ones about us women but consider how many and how much worse are the things he might have said and with truth, too." Mnesilochus begins to go into details but before the catalogue is complete he is mobbed by the women:

MICA. *How dare you plead for him who always chooses*
Such odious subjects for his plays, on purpose to abuse us;
Phaedras and Melanippes too: but ne'er a drama made he
About the good Penelope, or such-like virtuous lady.
MNESILOCHUS. *The cause I know; the cause I'll show: you won't discover any*
Penelopes alive today, but Phaedras very many.

The women suspect that they have a man among them. Mnesilochus is stripped, and his identity discovered. Then he is turned over to a Scythian policeman whose dialect is as barbarous as that spoken by his modern descendant.

In the *parabasis* of the play the women do not defend themselves against Euripides but merely accuse the men of inconsistency. " Why," they say, " if we are so bad are you so eager to marry us? "

*Everyone says we're a Plague, the source of all evils
    to man,*
*War, dissension and strife.   Come answer me this
    if you can;*
*Why, if we're really a Plague, you're so anxious to
    have us for wives;*
*And charge us not to be peeping, nor to stir out of
    doors for our lives.*
*Isn't it silly to guard a Plague with such scrupulous
    care?*

The concluding scenes of the play are parodies on Euripides' *Helen* and *Andromeda*.
Euripides tries to rescue his kinsman first in
the guise of Menelaus and later in the guise
of Perseus. The Scythian yields to Euripides'
pleading in neither of these characters but his
attention is diverted by a pretty chorus girl
who flirts with him. The play ends with the
escape of Mnesilochus and the fruitless en-
deavors of the Scythian to catch his charmer.
Of all the extant plays of Aristophanes this is
most like a modern play in having a consistent
and well-developed plot.

In 405 B.C. Aristophanes again made Euripides the subject of his ridicule in the *Frogs*.
Euripides and Sophocles had recently died
within a few months of each other and the

tragic stage was left now to second-rate artists. The great days of the tragedy were indeed over though Aristophanes could only surmise this. Dionysus is represented in the opening scene accompanied by his slave on a journey to the Lower World. He is tired of these second-rate poets and proposes to bring back to life Euripides, the popular idol. He has assumed the club and the lion skin of Heracles to be the better equipped on this fearsome journey. He stops to inquire of Heracles the route he had himself gone in his quest for Cerberus. Heracles tells Dionysus about the best inns where the bugs are fewest and speeds the god on his way in his absurd disguise.

The party soon encounter a dead man just being carried out to burial. Dionysus proposes to send a message in advance to Pluto but they cannot agree on the price for the service. The dead man is finally carried off in disgust, refusing to accept Dionysus' meager offer with the jibe: "I'd sooner come to life."

Terrified by the monsters on the way Dionysus forces his slave to exchange clothes with him. Arriving at Pluto's door the slave who has enjoyed playing the master refuses to give up his garments. Aeacus unable to tell which

is the real god has them whipped, being certain that a flogging will not hurt an immortal.
But both cry out at the blows, and in doubt
which is master and which is servant, Aeacus
sends them both in, assured that Pluto will
quickly know the difference.

The latter half of the play is taken up with
a contest between Aeschylus and Euripides to
decide which is the better poet. Sophocles has
resigned the tragic throne to Aeschylus, " for
he is gentle here as he was there." He says
that he will enter the combat against Euripides
if Aeschylus is worsted. Aeschylus objects
that the contest is unequal because while his
poetry is still alive on earth, Euripides' died
with him and is at hand for quotation. The
passages that follow form a brilliant series of
criticisms on Euripides' innovations in tragedy.
His prologues are found to be faulty because
of their monotony. The little phrase, " the
wine flask lost," can with disastrous results
be added as the second half of almost every
line. A great deal of sport is made of the
new melodies which Euripides introduced, of
his crafty turnings and new-fangled twists.
In despair Dionysus brings forth scales into
which each poet speaks in turn. The long

mouth-filling epithets of Aeschylus naturally outweigh the prettiness of Euripides' style. But the final test is: which poet has given better advice to the state. On this Aeschylus is easily judged superior and Dionysus prepares to lead him to the Upper World. "But," objects Euripides, "you swore to take me," to which Dionysus retorts with the famous line from the *Hippolytus* of Euripides, " 'Twas only my tongue that swore."

Strangely enough this play takes its name from a subordinate chorus composed of frogs. The monotonous " Brekekekex, ko-ax, ko-ax " of these frogs, croaking on the banks of the Styx, has survived in college yells. The main chorus, however, is composed of those who have been initiated into the mysteries of Demeter at Eleusis. Their songs are among the most brilliant of all Aristophanes' lyrics. They are, as a modern writer remarks, " fit for the most sacred ceremony of Eleusis."

Come, arise, from sleep awaking, come the fiery
    torches shaking,
O Iacchus, O Iacchus!
Morning star that shineth nightly,
Lo, the mead is blazing brightly,
Age forgets its years and sadness,

Aged knees curvet for gladness,
Lift thy shining torches o'er us,
Marshall all thy blameless train,
Lead, O lead the way before us; lead the lovely
  youthful chorus
To the marshy flowery plain.

It was such contrasts as these between the
solemn beauty of these noble songs and the
riotous revelry of the action that make the comedies of Aristophanes so unique and so impossible of imitation.

The contest between Euripides and Aeschylus in the *Frogs* is one of the very earliest and
one of the best documents in the whole history
of literary criticism. Aristophanes possessed,
as Saintsbury says: "both generally and in
this particular instance, all the requisites for
playing the part" (of literary critic) "to perfection, with one single exception — the possession, namely, of that wide comparative
knowledge of other literatures which the
Greeks lacked." [10]   The whole critique of both
poets is equally keen and, allowing for a strong
personal prejudice, surprisingly fair.   To have
produced such apt parodies of styles so different, to have noted with such unerring insight
the weakness and the power of each author

(for Euripides' defense is not weak), to have been concrete and vivid where Aristotle is only general and vague, in short to have produced the first great and influential document in literary criticism constitutes one of Aristophanes' claims to immortality.

Thirteen years passed before the next play of Aristophanes which is preserved appeared, the *Ecclesiazusae* or " The Women in Parliament." In those thirteen years many changes had taken place. Athens was no longer the proud mistress of the Aegean, her glory was departed and the old comedy with its keen political satire was beginning to be impossible. " The Women in Parliament " is a satire on women's rights. It is hard to believe that it is not a parody on the *Republic* of Plato, his ideal state in a part of which women are to have equal rights with men and where communism is to flourish. The date at which Plato's *Republic* was published seems to make impossible the belief that Aristophanes had that work definitely in mind, but there is so much in common between the two that one is tempted to believe that Aristophanes was acquainted with Plato's ideas and was, if the phrase may be used, " parodying in advance."

The principal character in the play is Praxagora. She is thoroughly tired of the way in which men are conducting the state, so she arranges a plot whereby the women may seize the reins of government. The opening scene displays a gathering of women at which they are rehearsing their parts. They plan to be at the Assembly when it opens, disguised in their husbands' garments. They are to pack the front rows and pass a resolution turning the entire state over to the women. Of course a rehearsal gives the poet an occasion to display many ludicrous slips. The women swear by the women's goddesses instead of by the gods and are rebuked by Praxagora. One woman almost betrays the plot by bringing her knitting.

The plot is successful and the entire charge of the government is given to the women. The state is then arranged by Praxagora on a purely communistic basis. All private property is to be done away with. The state supports everyone. Poverty and want are to be unknown. Thieves will go out of business, "for why should they steal what is partly their own." Gambling is abolished for no man has anything to stake. All wives are to be in common and children will be reared by the state. Reverence will naturally be given to old men, for no child would dare show disrespect to a person who might, for all he knew, be his father. The law courts are abandoned and in their stead banqueting booths are arranged. The latter part of the play is filled with scenes of wild indecency in which the communism of wives is illustrated. The comedy ends with a hilarious dance by the Chorus as they go out to the banquet which the chieftainess has prepared. The Chorus plays a much less important part than in the earlier plays and the *parabasis* is entirely lacking.

The only other extant comedy of Aristophanes is the *Plutus*, produced first in 408 B.C. and in a revised edition in 388 B.C. It is the latter edition which has survived. This play lacks the riotous fancy and the brilliant repartee of the earlier comedies. The poet's genius had evidently spent itself. The changed political conditions had created an atmosphere unfavorable to the earlier freedom of speech and instead of the keen personal, political or literary satire we have merely a dramatized allegory.

The god of wealth, Plutus, who has been

blinded that he may not rule the world, has been captured by a citizen of Athens, Chremylus. He is taken to the shrine of the god Aesculapius and there healed. This gives the poet a chance to satirize the practices of the temple priests and the gullibility of human nature in general. These scenes are the best part of the play. Now that his sight is restored the god proceeds to enrich the deserving and impoverish the malefactors. The Chorus has still further declined. There are few songs in this play and no *parabasis*. The old comedy is indeed passing away.

Aristophanes was first of all a comic poet. He was interested in winning the prize of comedy and to do this he must entertain his audience. It is a mistake to regard him chiefly as a statesman influencing the citizens through the medium of comedy. He was rather a comic poet very much interested in the welfare of his city. That he was the most successful comic poet of his day is the universal testimony of antiquity; and the fact that his plays have survived is in itself a proof that they were more cherished than those of his contemporaries. During his long life with few

reverses he held the first place on the comic
stage. His influence on the development of
comedy was paramount. In the *parabasis* of
the *Peace* he boasts, and his boasting cannot
be denied, that it was he who elevated the
comedy from rude and coarse buffoonery to an
artistic performance:

I*t was he that indignantly swept from the stage*
the paltry ignoble device
O*f a Heracles needy and seedy and greedy, a vaga-*
bond sturdy and stout,
N*ow baking his bread, now swindling instead, now*
beaten and battered about.
A*nd freedom he gave to the lachrymose slave who*
was wont with a howl to rush in,
A*nd all for the sake of a joke which they make on*
the wounds that disfigure the skin;
"W*hy, how now, my poor knave?" so they bawl*
to the slave, "has the whipcord invaded your
back,
S*preading havoc around, hacking trees to the*
ground, with a savage resistless attack?"
S*uch vulgar contemptible lumber at once he bade*
from the drama depart,
A*nd then like an edifice stately and grand, he*
raised and ennobled the Art.
H*igh thoughts and high language he brought on*
the stage, a humour exalted and rare,

N*or stooped with a scurrilous jest to assail some
    small man and woman affair.*
N*o, he at the mightiest quarry of all with the soul
    of a Heracles flew,*
A*nd he braved the vile scent of the tan-pit, and
    went through foul-mouthed revilings for you.*

It is impossible to doubt that Aristophanes
in his endeavor to refine comedy went as far
as he could, even further on some occasions
than his audience would follow him. The
Clouds and the *Birds* both failed to receive
first prize apparently because of their lack of
that broad buffoonery and ribaldry to which
the Athenian audience was so partial. In each
case in the succeeding play the poet was compelled to restore the wanton scenes which the
audience demanded and on which his success
depended.

It is quite as wide of the mark, however, to
regard Aristophanes merely as a comic poet
as it is to regard him as a statesman in disguise. He was deeply interested in the state
and his best comedies show him in the light
of a constructive conservative partisan. For
he is always conservative. In fact this is almost a necessary characteristic of the humorist,
who usually finds his mark in attacking the in-

novator. But with Aristophanes it is more than the mere accident of a humorous situation that caused him on every occasion " to abhor what is new and to choose what is old." It was the old education, the old poetry, and the old political oligarchical system that appealed to him. He loved Aeschylus who sang of the men who fought at Marathon, he abhorred Euripides with his innovations and his rhetorical sophistication. He believed in the old stereotyped education and regarded the elective system of the sophists as a desolation and a hissing. And with all his conservatism he was a safe guide for the Athenian people. How often his prophecies were fulfilled and his advice justified! His attacks on Cleon and Hyperbolus were thoroughly deserved if we may trust the judgment of historians, ancient and modern. While he is not fair to Euripides the strictures which he makes on his plays are often justified. Euripides is judged by the nineteen plays which have survived and usually by the best six or seven. What would the verdict be now if it were possible to review, as Aristophanes could, all of those undoubtedly inferior plays which have perished? A careful analysis even of those which are extant leaves the student with a greater confidence in the justice of Aristophanes' indictments.

But aside from his distinction as a comedian and as a statesman, Aristophanes is one of the greatest poets the world has ever seen. Nowhere else, even in the great tragedians, does the true note of lyric poetry ring so clear. The serenade of the Hoopoe to the Nightingale in the *Birds* is not unworthy of the bird " that sings in the inviolate bowers of the god at White Colonus ":

Awake my mate!
Shake off thy slumbers, and clear and strong
Let loose the floods of thy glorious song,
The sacred dirge of thy mouth divine
For sore-wept Itys, thy child and mine;
Thy tender thrillings his name prolong
With the liquid note of thy tawny throat;
Through the leafy curls of the woodbine sweet
The pure sound mounts to the heavenly seat,
And Phoebus lord of the golden hair,
As he lists to thy wild plaint echoing there,
Draws answering strains from his ivoried lyre,
Till he stirs the dance of the heavenly choir,
And calls from the blessed lips on high
Of immortal gods, a divine reply
To the tones of thy witching melody. (Vs. 209–
222)

The long anapaestic meter which Swinburne calls "his marvelous metrical invention," so fluently rendered by Mr. Rogers, is enough to have made any poet famous. The play of his poetic fancy is as whimsical and as winning as that of Shakespeare, and he could invest, even in parody, the dry cosmography of the philosophers with a poetic beauty which Lucretius could not equal. Where in literature can one find the lines to match the great chorus of the *Birds* which begins:

*Ye men who are dimly existing below, who perish
    and fade as the leaf,*
*Pale, woebegone, shadowlike, spiritless folk, life
    feeble and wingless and brief,*
*Frail castings in clay, who are gone in a day, like
    a dream full of sorrow and sighing,*
*Come listen with care to the Birds of the air, the
    ageless, the deathless, who flying*
*In the joy and the freshness of Ether, are wont to
    muse upon wisdom undying.*
*We will tell you of things transcendental; of
    Springs and of Rivers the mighty upheaval;*
*The nature of Birds; and the birth of the Gods;
    and of Chaos and Darkness primeval.*
*When this ye shall know, let old Prodicus go, and
    be hanged without hope of reprieval.*

*There was Chaos at first, and Darkness and Night
    and Tartarus vasty and dismal;*
*But the Earth was not there, nor the Sky, nor the
    Air, till at length in the bosom abysmal*
*Of Darkness an egg, from the whirlwind conceived,
    was laid by the sable plumed Night.*
*And out of that egg, as the Seasons revolved,
    sprang Love, the entrancing, the bright,*
*Love brilliant and bold with his pinions of gold,
    like a whirlwind, refulgent and sparkling!*
*Love hatched us, commingling in Tartarus wide,
    with Chaos, the murky, the darkling,*
*And brought us above, as the firstlings of love, and
    first to the light we ascended.*
*There was never a race of Immortals at all till
    Love had the universe blended;*
*Then all things commingling together in love, there
    arose the fair Earth and the sky,*
*And the limitless Sea; and the race of the Gods,
    the blessed, who never shall die.*

Perhaps the unexpectedness of these poetical
passages adds a great deal to their charm.
One instance will suffice. It is from the
Clouds, the passage in which the Right Argument hopes to persuade Pheidippides to choose
the good old education. The Argument says:

*But then you'll excell in the games you love well,
    all blooming, athletic and fair:*

[70]

*Not learning to prate as your elders debate with
    marvelous prickly dispute,*
*Nor dragged into court day by day to make sport
    in some small disagreeable suit:*
*But you will below to the Academe go, and under
    the olive contend*
*With your chaplet of reed, in a contest of speed
    with some excellent rival and friend:*
*All fragrant with woodbine and peaceful content,
    and the leaf which the lime blossoms fling,*
*When the plane whispers love to the elm in the
    grove in the beautiful season of Spring.* (Vs.
1002–1008)

From the tedious wrangle over educational methods, we are transported at once and completely to the fair grove of Academus with its olive trees, its whispering pines, its spreading plane trees and its towering elms through which the breezes of Spring flit carrying messages of love.

There is in Aristophanes too an unexpected gentleness and a quality akin to tears. It is that feeling " of brooding pity " which Mr. Mackail so sympathetically describes in his discussion of the *Aeneid* and which Pliny [11] almost apprehends when he speaks of the *dulcedo,* " the poignancy " of the Old Comedy.

The *lacrimae rerum* are never far from his
thoughts and the laugh of the jester often ends
in a choking sob. So he wistfully speaks of
Sophocles, recently dead,[12] in the House of
Hades: "He is gentle here and gentle he was
there." In the *Lysistrata* an Athenian Magistrate is arguing that women should have nothing to say in the decisions of the State for war
or peace:

LYS: *Nothing to do with it, wretch that you are!*
We are the people who feel it the keenliest, doubly
　　on us the affliction is cast;
Where are the sons that we sent to your battle-
　　fields? (They were lying dead by the thou-
　　sands in the olive groves of Sicily and the
　　quarries of Syracuse.)
MAGISTRATE: *Silence! a truce to the ills of the*
　　past.
LYS: *Then in the glory and the grace of our*
　　womanhood, all in the May and the morning
　　of life,
Lo we are sitting, forlorn and disconsolate, what
　　has a soldier to do with a wife?
We might endure it, but ah! for the younger ones,
　　still in their maiden apartments they stay,
Wanting the husband that never approaches them,
　　watching the years that are gliding away.

MAGISTRATE: *Men, I suppose, have their youth
   everlastingly.*
LYS: *Nay, but it isn't the same with a man;*
*Grey though he be when he comes from the battle-
   field,*
Still if he wishes to marry, he can.
*Brief is the spring and the flower of our woman-
   hood, once let it slip, and it comes not again;*
*Sit as we may with our spells and our auguries,
   never a husband will marry us then.*

No Greek poet, not even Sophocles, has more
tenderly dealt with maidenhood's "short season." And the passage is all the more moving
because in the very next lines as if ashamed of
his momentary pathos, Aristophanes passes to
a scene of wild revelry in which the Magistrate
is decked out as a corpse for burial.

The survival of Aristophanes' plays alone
among the writers of Old Comedy is one of
the proofs of his preëminence otherwise so
abundantly attested. Of his professional success he was undoubtedly jealous and proud.
But the most gratifying distinction conferred
on him was the presentation of a wreath of
wild olive made from the leaves of Athena's
own sacred olive tree on the Acropolis. This
was awarded him on the second performance

of the *Frogs*, not because of his glorious poetry or his sparkling wit, not because he was an artist or a humorist, but because he had given the city patriotic advice. He had counselled the citizens that, in view of the stern crisis they were facing, they should, foregoing party rivalry, forgetting their feuds and their narrow jealousy, recall the exiles to their homes and re-enfranchise them. The statesman had transcended the poet, or rather through the poet's art a great Athenian patriot had spoken, and it was the statesman who had given such advice at the risk of his own position whom the city had splendidly honored.

IV. ARISTOPHANES' INFLUENCE ON GREECE AND ROME

IT is difficult to gauge with correctness the influence which Aristophanes exercised on his own generation. His influence as a literary artist is particularly hard to estimate, for the plays of his contemporaries exist only in scattered fragments. It is quite clear that he found the comedy well developed, that he did not change its essential character by any remarkable innovations. It is quite certain that he did much to elevate comedy from mere horse play and rude personal satire to a thoughtful criticism of government policies and of tendencies in philosophy and literature. It is equally certain that he carried this improvement of comedy as far as the taste of his audiences would allow and even further. The *Wasps* would have been a better play if the judges had approved of the *Clouds*.

It is much easier to trace Aristophanes' influence on the political life of the time. Here we find that he is accurate as an historian and that he foresees with astonishing clearness coming political events. He is never mentioned by Thucydides — nor is Aeschylus or Sophocles or Euripides. But his plays that deal with the Peloponnesian War are remarkable for their agreement with the *History* of Thucydides. So close is the similarity of the language employed that it has been suggested that Thucydides used Aristophanes' plays as one of his sources. However this may be, one who forms his ideas of the life at Athens during this struggle, from Aristophanes' plays would not go far wrong. It is a mere matter of coincidence that he should have foretold the very manner of Lamachus' death, but it is no mere accident that he should have drawn so clear a picture of the two generals, Demosthenes and Nicias, or that Cleomenes and Theramenes should have been done true to life. Cleisthenes too is an accurate portrait. Again, Aristophanes truthfully predicted that Hyperbolus would succeed Cleon in the favor of the Assembly; and the impending revolution is foretold in the prayer raised by the Chorus of the *Thesmophoriazusae* to " Pallas, the Hater of Tyranny."

These are instances where Aristophanes

seems by inspiration or chance to predict the
future. But it may fairly be urged that the
Peace had a potent influence in bringing about
the Peace of Nicias which was signed not long
after. It has been seen how the State thanked
him for the advice given in the *Frogs* in favor
of enfranchising the exiles — advice that was
taken. It is quite likely that many regretted
that they did not take the equally sound advice which he gave in favor of discarding Cleon
and making peace after the defeat of the Spartans at Sphacteria and Pylos. How fortunate
it would have been for Athens if she had taken
his advice (*praeceptum altioris prudentiae*) [13]
about the treatment of Alcibiades:

> *'Twere best to rear no lion in the state;*
> *But having reared, 'tis best to humor him.*

How influential his caricature of Socrates
was has already been noted. It is not fanciful to believe that one of the influences which
kept Euripides from winning the tragic prize
except on rare occasions was the sturdy battle
which Aristophanes waged in and out of season against the innovations which Euripides
was employing to "popularize" the Attic
tragedy. What other reason could be given

why this gifted poet was so unsuccessful with
the Athenian judges during his lifetime and
the lifetime of Aristophanes, and so much preferred to Sophocles and Aeschylus by the
Greek cities of Sicily during the latter part
of his own life and by all Hellas in the generation that followed Aristophanes' death?

In the days when Greek literature had become a subject of learned study, comedy was
divided into three divisions, the Old Comedy,
the Middle, and the New. In the Middle
Comedy the attack was aimed at tendencies
and ideas rather than at individuals. It is to
this class that the *Plutus* of Aristophanes belongs. With all the prestige that his long and
successful career lent him it was impossible
to continue the intensely personal satire that
the Old Comedy demanded. Such a drama
could only flourish or even be tolerated in a
democracy as free as fifth century Athens.
Among equals one might say what he thought
of his neighbor but no oligarchy will tolerate
personal comments from the groundlings. So
swift was the rise and the passing of this
unique literary form, the Old Comedy, that
the life of a single individual might have witnessed its entire course. The Middle Comedy

with its travesties of mythological scenes and philosophical tenets gave way to the New Comedy of Philemon, Diphilus and Menander. The New Comedy is a comedy of manners and differs little from the comedy of the present day, allowing for differences of time and custom. It is a comedy of intrigue, adventure and love. It is from this comedy and not the Old Comedy that the French, the German and the English comedy is derived.

Aristophanes' latest plays belonged to Middle Comedy but on the New Comedy he had little influence. It is true that many of the devices of the New Comedy are taken from Aristophanes and the Old Comedy. The recognition scene, the soliloquy, the aside, the parasite, and the sycophant are all part of Aristophanes' machinery, but to believe that the New Comedians consciously went back to him for inspiration is a mistake. They drew rather upon the life about them, which Menander so perfectly reflects. The praise of Peace which occurs in one of the fragments of his plays and the passage discussing the education of the good old times are more likely to come from a study of the conversation of the *laudatores temporis acti* than from a study of the Old Comedy. It is elsewhere that one must look for the influence of Aristophanes.

Plato's attitude toward Aristophanes personally is hard to determine, his attitude toward his art is one of condemnation. Yet there is a tradition that Plato recommended Aristophanes to his pupil Dionysius, the youthful tyrant of Syracuse. In the *Symposium* he represents Aristophanes discoursing on Love. The great comedian could not have done it better. It is hard to believe that this whimsical description of the curious four-legged, four-handed human beings who ran by rapidly rolling over like a tumbler, throwing hand springs, and who were cleft apart by Zeus and repaired by Apollo — it is hard to believe that this is all from Plato's imagination and not an account of an actual conversation with Aristophanes. It has every ear mark of the poet's mind, his riotous fancy, his plausibility, his sudden flashes of poetry.

Plato in the *Apology* represents Socrates blaming Aristophanes more than anyone else for the misconception of his teaching prevalent among the Athenians. Yet in the *Symposium* they are on the best of terms and that dialogue closes with Agathon, the tragic poet,

Aristophanes and Socrates — the only revelers still awake at dawn — still arguing over the nature of tragedy and comedy. "Socrates was insisting to the other two that the genius of comedy was the same as that of tragedy, and that the writer of tragedy ought to be a writer of comedy also. To this they were compelled to assent, being sleepy, and not quite understanding his meaning. And first of all Aristophanes dropped and then when the day was already dawning, Agathon. Socrates, when he had put them to sleep, rose to depart." [14]

In Plato's mind tragedy and comedy are essentially the same — both are "imitations" as Aristotle also later called them. And as imitations or representations of what is so often unworthy they are to be banished from the Ideal State. Familiarity with these representations gradually accustoms the audience to look without condemnation on reprehensible acts. And in the comedy particularly the laughter and approval with which the misfortunes of others are greeted dulls the sympathy of the spectators and has a deleterious effect on their morals. The passions of love, anger, fear, jealousy are all unworthy and should not afford pleasure. Aristophanes' comedy is therefore along with tragedy excluded from Plato's Ideal Republic.

Aristotle does not approve of Aristophanes. The language of the Old Comedy seems to him coarse and harsh, it lacks the " delicate innuendo " of the later works, it is too personal. The reason for Aristotle's preference is not far to seek. It is not due so much to his own association with monarchs like Philip and Alexander who would have tolerated anything rather than such freedom of speech as the Old Comedy allowed, as it is to his own desire for generalization. " Poetry aims at complete universality and achieves it when the poet constructs his plots on lines of probability and then inserts characteristic names." The Old Comedy did this in a greater degree than Aristotle thought. To a certain extent Socrates, Euripides, and Cleon are types, representative of tendencies in which Aristophanes did not believe, but they were also individual objects of the poet's attack — especially Cleon. But the Middle and the New Comedy, the complete development of which he did not live to see, fulfilled Aristotle's requirements of generalization completely. In fact as they stand they appeal almost as much to a modern audience as they did when first produced. But to enjoy with anything like completeness a play of Aristophanes requires much information about the local conditions under which it was written. The plots of the New Comedy are probable, the names are characteristic and the result is complete universality and hence poetry, for " Poetry is a more philosophical and a higher thing than history; for poetry tends to express the universal, history the particular." [15]

Four hundred years later Plutarch expressed a somewhat similar judgment about Aristophanes. Plutarch, who deprecated the fact that the Athenians spent funds on the production of plays that might better have been employed in the maintenance of a military establishment and who thought Herodotus " malignant " because he told the truth about the treachery of Thebes in the Persian wars, prefers Menander to Aristophanes. The latter, he says, has a sordid and theatrical mode of expression which offends a cultured person. The language is not fitted to the character who speaks. Aristophanes is coarse and harsh. He has an angry and biting sharpness. His characters are overdrawn; his clowns are not jocose but ridiculous; his lovers not gay, but lewd. His style is a patchwork of tragic and comic, of pretentious and commonplace, of obscure and simple. Menander is clear and direct and even in those passages where caricature is absent his dialogue is more true to life.

That Plutarch's fine sensibilities should have been offended by Aristophanes' coarseness is not strange, that he should have found Menander more realistic in the commonplaceness of his dialogue is not surprising, for it is true, but that he should have missed the high moral tone, the ardent patriotism and the glorious poetry of Aristophanes goes far toward justifying the poor opinion which Macaulay held of his acumen.[16] " Indeed, the manner of Plutarch reminds us of the cookery of those continental inns, the horror of English travellers, in which a certain nondescript broth is kept constantly boiling, and copiously poured without distinction over every dish as it comes up to table." What can be thought of a critic who turns from Aristophanes' plays and in sheer bewilderment inquires: " Now will someone please tell me what there was funny about that? "

When the creative impulse of the Greek literary genius had spent itself and Theocritus with his Sicilian shepherd's pipe was the only clear voiced minstrel of the muses, it was natural that Aristophanes should, among others, become the subject of learned commentaries. At Alexandria and at Pergamum he was eagerly studied by the learned denizens of those great libraries — though he can not be said to have influenced those worthies greatly. If he had there might have been more of the joy of life in their works. His plays, however, from their very local nature needed much explanation and the long line of distinguished scholars who made him the subject of their treatises is clear proof that he was one of the "seven-day books" most in demand at the great libraries.

Lycophron who was called to the library at Alexandria about 285 B.C. to arrange the comic poets seems to have been the first to write a commentary — and not a good one either — on Aristophanes. Not much later Callimachus wrote a series of lives of the poets — including the writers of comedy with the dates of the production of the plays. But the first great contribution to the elucidation of the many

doubtful questions in Aristophanes' poems was
made by Eratosthenes, librarian at Alexandria
234–195 B.C. He corrected many of the mistakes made by Lycophron and Callimachus.
His successor Aristophanes of Byzantium
(librarian 195–180 B.C.), is, however, the great
and ultimate source of the commentaries on
the Attic Comedy. He published an edition
of Aristophanes with a commentary and introduction to each play. These introductions
in abbreviated form are still extant. Two of
his pupils, Aristarchus (librarian 180–146
B.C.) and Callistratus, continued these studies
and added valuable commentaries. And in
Pergamum, Crates of Mallus by his labors of
elucidation testified to the universal interest
in the great Attic Comedy writer.

No great addition was made to the work of
these scholars till the time of Didymus, who
because of his prodigious capacity for work
was given the complimentary rather than elegant nickname of " brass guts " (*chalcenterus*).
He lived at Alexandria in the Augustan age
collecting and editing the work of former
scholars. The ancient comments on the plays
which have survived — the scholia — are
largely his revisions of the great commentary

of Aristophanes of Byzantium further revised
one hundred years later by Symmachus. Much
later in Byzantium the didactic poet Tzetzes
(1150 A.D.) and Anna Comnena, the sister of
John II, the best of the Emperors of the East,
were familiar with Aristophanes as their writ-
ings show.

Even in the days of imperial Rome when
the studio tragedies of Seneca and the artificial
epics of Statius and Silius Italicus were only
partially relieved by the pungent *Satires* of
Juvenal, when the chief occupation of the
man about town was to join his friends
each afternoon in listening to prize compositions till the oratory fairly shattered the pillars of the porticoes, — even in this age the
Younger Pliny could praise his friend Vergilius
Romanus for the composition of a comedy in
the old Attic style and could characterize that
style in such a way that it is clear that he must
have been familiar with Aristophanes and have
appreciated him. Dignity, subtlety, keenness,
poignancy, charm, are the terms used by
Pliny [17] to describe the Old Comedy. Two
hundred and fifty years later the Emperor
Julian prided himself on his familiarity with
Aristophanes; and Aristophanes' popularity is

further attested by two epigrams of the first Christian century. Diodorus of Sardis writes: "Divine Aristophanes lies dead beneath me. If thou askest which, it is the comic poet who keeps the memory of the old stage alive," [18] and Antipater of Thessalonica ends a fine epitaph on Aristophanes' works with: "O Comic poet, high of heart and worthy interpreter of the spirit of Hellas, hating what deserved hate and mocking where mockery was due." [19]

But a more convincing proof of Aristophanes' influence can be given. Under all of Aristophanes' criticism of Euripides, as Mr. Butcher noted, there lies a moral idea. Euripides is a bad poet because he makes bad citizens. Aristotle's standard is quite different; he judges poetry on "aesthetic and logical grounds." [20] That is, he applies to Euripides' plays exactly the standards that would now be used in judging their poetical value. It would be natural to expect that the early scholars who wrote commentaries on Euripides would have used the material for criticism of his plays lying ready to hand in Aristotle's thoughtful work on the *Theory of Poetry;* but not so. There is hardly a trace of its influence in the older Euripidean scholia, while Aristophanes' criticisms are familiar ground and his standards of criticism are adopted. The earlier commentators find with Aristophanes that Euripides is a maker of beggars, a rhetorician, that his characters are not differentiated, that he is clever and not clear, fond of genealogies and a hater of women. Thus the great patriot-poet's influence began first to be felt as a literary critic.

When after five hundred years of struggle and warfare Rome at last turned her thoughts toward literature, comedy was almost her first production. There had been a native comedy but this was supplemented by translations and adaptations from the Greek. With the three types of Greek Comedy before them as models the Romans might conceivably have chosen to imitate any one of them. A revival of the Old Comedy at Rome would have added a gaiety and sprightliness to their literature which it conspicuously lacks. There is a story that such a revival was attempted which if not historically accurate has at least a deeper poetical truth. Gnaeus Naevius, the second poet of Rome, wrote a comedy in the style of the Greek poets in which he paid his respects to the Metelli, one of the leading patrician fam-

ilies. He said among other things that it was
by fate (and by no merit of their own) that
the Metelli were consuls at Rome. To which
the Metelli replied in verse that " The Metelli
will make it hot for the poet, Naevius " [21] —
which they proceeded to do. He was thrown
into prison till — as the story goes — he re-
canted. Later he was exiled and died in Af-
rica. This experience naturally " sicklied o'er
with the pale cast of thought " the spirits of
those who were inclined to write Aristophanic
comedy at Rome. Indeed the idea of indulg-
ing freely in personalities on the stage was ab-
horrent to Roman dignity, at least to the dignity of the first families who controlled the
government and who would also be recipients
of these personalities. The matter is well put
by Cicero: " Among them (the older Greeks)
comedy was allowed by law to say what it
wished, of whom it pleased by name. . . .
Whom did it not touch or rather whom did it
not attack? Whom did it spare? Well, it attacked men of the common herd, disagreeable
fellows, a nuisance to the state, Cleon, Cleo-
phon, Hyperbolus. We might put up with that,
although it were better that citizens of this type
be branded by the censor than by a poet. But

it was no more fitting that Pericles, after he had for very many years with very great influence led his state at home and abroad, should be attacked in poetry and dragged on the stage than it would have been if our poets Plautus or Naevius had assailed Publius and Gnaeus Scipio or if Caecilius had slandered Marcus Cato. . . . Though our laws of the Twelve Tables have prescribed the death penalty for few things, among these death was decreed to anyone who should sing a lampoon or publish a poem which was slanderous or charged another person with a crime." [22]

The incident of Naevius is more important because it shows how the Roman comedy was thrown back from an imitation of Aristophanes to adaptation of the plays of Menander, Philemon and the other writers of the New Comedy. But there was another branch of Latin literature where Aristophanes' influence was to be supreme, that branch which is regarded even by Quintilian as entirely Roman — the Satire.

Lucilius, the first great Roman Satirist, wrote on a great variety of subjects some of which did not lend themselves to satire as the term is now used. Some of his satires were merely narratives filled with wit and anecdotes.

But in many of his poems he attacks the customs of the men of his time with all the vigor of Aristophanes. Horace says that he laid violent hands on the leading citizens and the people, a whole tribe at a time, that he scoured down the city with strong brine, [23] and Juvenal compares him to a man in a passion with his sword drawn from its sheath. [24]

Lucilius owed his immunity from prosecution to the fact that he was a man of high social standing — Latin equestrian rank — and that he kept out of politics himself, but even more to the protecting aegis of the powerful literary coterie of Scipio and Laelius to which he belonged. His personal attacks had all the virulence of Aristophanes; in matters of public morality and state policy he showed something of the same high-mindedness and from some of the fragments of his works which have survived it would seem that he had a similar conception of the importance of his task.

Horace emphasizes — doubtless over-emphasizes — this dependence of Lucilius on Aristophanes. He says: " Eupolis and Cratinus and Aristophanes and the other poets who wrote Old Comedy with much freedom branded any one who deserved to be satirized because he was a rascal and robber or adulterer or assassin or infamous for any other reason —upon these Lucilius is entirely dependent except for his meters." [25] Horace avows himself in satire a follower of Lucilius and so of the Old Comedy. He regards Lucilius as a careless artist, forceful but slovenly. It is not enough for a satirist to be vigorous, he must have besides a style characterized by brevity, now serious, now light, suited alike to the orator, to the poet and to the polished city wit. Though Horace thus acknowledges the influence of Aristophanes, though he is an avowed follower of the Old Comedy, his satires soon lose their tone of personal invective and become to all intents a reflection of the New Comedy. His genius had more of the urbane humor of Menander than the brilliant wit of Aristophanes and his good-natured irony shrank from the passions of invective in which Lucilius could indulge.

A generation later Aristophanes was still the ideal of the Satirist. Persius, that curious compound of ignorance and wisdom, of inexperience and insight, was inspired to write his six remarkable satires by reading Lucilius and he definitely claims for his audience those few who have a relish for the Old Comedy of Greece. [26] It must be confessed that he too fell far short of his model; but it is to the Athenian poet's passion for justice that he owes his vindictive morality; his involved obscurity is all his own.

Juvenal who lived about one hundred years after Horace still looks back to Lucilius as his model. He does not expressly say that he is following the Attic Comedies of Aristophanes' time but in spirit he is nearer to them than either Horace or Persius. He has a directness of expression and a grim sincerity of purpose that remind one of Aristophanes' personal attacks. And while Juvenal's victims are often safe in the tomb before the bolt falls, the vividness of his invective is almost elemental in its nature.

Thus all the great Satirists of Rome drew their inspiration from Aristophanes and his fellow dramatists. Quintilian might proudly claim that Satire was entirely a Roman creation, but its authors dutifully acknowledge their obligations. This is Aristophanes' second great contribution — the guiding inspiration in Roman Satire.

Meanwhile Aristophanes' influence was being felt in a most unexpected quarter. He had criticized Euripides unsparingly for his rhetorical innovations and his argumentative cleverness. It was a peculiar bit of poetic irony that Aristophanes should himself have become a model in the schools of rhetoric and, what was worse, that he should have often been recommended to students along with Euripides. Times had certainly changed! The author of the treatise *On the Sublime,* the first writer who brought to his work on literary criticism a knowledge of the stylistic value of the Old Testament, says: [27] "We have, however, sufficiently shown that many writers and poets who possess no natural ability and are perhaps even wanting in elevation have nevertheless, although employing for the most part common and popular words with no striking associations of their own, by merely joining and fitting these together, secured dignity and distinction and the appearance of freedom from meanness. Instances will be furnished by Philistus among many others, by Aristophanes in certain passages, by Euripides in most."

> *An tua demens*
> *Vilibus in ludis dictari carmina malis?*
> *Non ego.*[28]

But the most striking proof of the value set upon Aristophanes as a model for the young orator is furnished by that most sane of all Roman critics, Quintilian. In the time of Domitian out of his ripe experience as a lawyer and a teacher he compiled a work on the *Training of the Orator*. In the course of this he gives a brief résumé of Greek and Roman literature, noting the qualities in each author which may make him valuable for the student of oratory:[29] " The Old Comedy is almost the only form of poetry which preserves intact the true grace of Attic diction, while it is characterized by the most eloquent freedom of speech and shows especial power in the denunciation of vice; but it reveals great force in other departments as well. For its style is at once lofty, elegant and graceful, and if we except Homer, who like Achilles among warriors is beyond all comparison, I am not sure that there is any style which bears a closer resemblance to oratory or is better adapted for forming the orator. There are a number of writers of the Old Comedy, but the best are Aristophanes, Eupolis and Cratinus." Later,[30] speaking of the ineptness of Roman Comedy he adds: " Indeed, it seems to me as though the language of Rome were incapable of reproducing that graceful wit which was granted to Athens alone and was beyond the reach of other Greek dialects to achieve."

We know that Aristophanes prided himself on the purity of his language, that happy mean alike removed from the over-refinement of the city purists and the crude speech of the countrymen. He did not even deny the charge of his contemporaries that there was a dash of Euripides' style sprinkled in. It was this graceful and flexible style that Quintilian coveted for the narrative portions of an oration, while the flaming wrath of his denunciations and his moral earnestness were a model for the impassioned peroration.

In the light of this praise of Quintilian it is not so hard to believe a story which comes from a much later date. In the *editio princeps* of Aristophanes published in 1498, Aldo Manuzio says that St. John Chrysostom was so fond of Aristophanes that he constantly had with him a copy of twenty-eight of his plays, that he always put them beneath his pillow at night, as Alexander his Homer, and that to his constant study of this poet he owed his unmatched eloquence and his hatred of vice. The story is quite circumstantial and is repeated elsewhere. Porson, the great English scholar whose feeling for the niceties of Greek style has perhaps never been excelled, thought he could find traces of direct imitation of Aristophanes in St. John. The case is not a clear one. Of the seventeen extra plays included in the twenty-eight comedies mentioned by Aldo no trace has been found. St. Chrysostom was particularly noted for his austere life and his scathing denunciation of all declension from the highest standards of moral rectitude. His very surname, "He of the Golden Lips," testifies to his eloquence. As Quintilian thought Aristophanes the best model for impassioned denunciation St. John may well have accepted his advice — he could have had no better guide. In doubtful cases of this kind it is often comforting to accept Livy's easy principles: "In matters so ancient if anything is probable, I should be satisfied to accept it as truth." [31]

It is no part of the purpose of this sketch to collect or to mention all the references to Aristophanes in classical literature. He is cited copiously by technical writers, and grammarians delight in writing glosses on his rare words. Admiration is the universal note —

to Cicero and Aulus Gellius alike he is " *face-tissimus.*"

Before the spring of Greek literature failed, there was born (about 120 A.D.) at Samosata on the Euphrates a man who was to recall the spirit and genius of Aristophanes, Lucian. He was a writer of essays and the inventor of a new literary form — the dialogue for amusement — as he called it, a union of dialogue and comedy. Dialogues hitherto had been used for purposes of serious exposition — the philosophical essay was a dialogue. Comedy was for the stage. Lucian conceived the idea of writing dialogues in the comic style to be read, not produced. It was not a long step from the literary mime, but apparently no one had made that step from verse to prose. Lucian, as he is the first in time, is still the first in excellence of the writers of imaginary dialogue.

Some of these dialogues are inspired by the cynic philosopher Menippus, some like the *Dialogues of the Courtesans* come from the New Comedy, but the most interesting collection is drawn from the Aristophanic comedy. Mons. Croiset assigns the following to the influence of the Old Comedy writers: (a) Satires on the vanity of human wishes, *A Voyage to the Lower World,* a dialogue on the vanity of power; *Charon,* a dialogue on the vanity of all things; *Timon,* a dialogue on the vanity of riches; *The Cock,* a dialogue on the vanity of riches and power. (b) Satires on religion, *Prometheus on Caucasus, Zeus Tragoedus, The Gods in Council.* (c) Satires on philosophers, *The Ship,* a dialogue on foolish aspirations; *Life of Peregrine* and *The Runaways,* satires on the Cynics; *The Double Indictment* and the *Fisher,* autobiographic dialogues, and the *Sale of Creeds,* a satire on philosophers.[32]

Besides these there are references to Aristophanes in Lucian's other dialogues, direct and indirect, too numerous to be catalogued here. In *How to Write History,* mindful of Aristophanes' bold attack on Cleon, he says: " Cleon, the all-powerful in the assembly, shall not make him (the historian) afraid," and in *A True King* the hero actually visits Peisthetaerus' " city of Cloudcuckooborough." The *True Story* — a parody on the *Odyssey* and the model for *Gulliver's Travels* — is an account of a fabulous journey to the Isle of the Blessed, the Moon and many other interesting places. It shows the true spirit of Aristophanes in its extravagant imagination and its whimsical satire.

Lucian, more than any other Greek writer, caught the spirit of the great Comedian. But while in his brilliance, his graceful style, suiting itself easily to the proper characters of the several speakers, his facile grace, his wit and his prolific imagination he resembles the Athenian he lacks that quality for which Aristophanes is most prized — his wholesome laughter. Lucian is after all a cynic, and cynical irony in large doses is distressing. Brilliance and wit can dazzle for an afternoon, but they soon bring satiety and the reader is glad to withdraw from the presence of that mocking cynical smile and those mordant satires to the sunshine and the free air of Aristophanes' rippling mirth and honest hatreds.

V. ARISTOPHANES AND THE RENAISSANCE

HOMER, the sovereign poet, Horace, the Satirist, Ovid and Lucan, — these with his master Virgil and himself made for Dante the six supreme poets. Aristophanes is never mentioned by him, nor is Sophocles nor Aeschylus. But in spite of this fact many similarities between the works of the Athenian and the Florentine have been noted by Professor Zuretti.[33] Each made the politics of a small city a matter of universal interest. Each had his ideal in the past and strove to reproduce it in the future. Both were censors of their fellow men. Their poetry is individual but their interest is universal. Their attacks are directed against persons but their message is for the state. Their very censoriousness, their aloofness, make their appeal universal. Aristophanes' political ideal was peace, Dante's, the Empire. Neither was personally ambitious, though politics was the supreme interest of each. Alike they avoided tragedy because it would relegate them to the mythical or legendary past — away from the present in which each found his supreme interest. Incidentally, each was a distinguished literary critic. Whether or not Dante was a student of Aristophanes is a question that can not be answered. There is no evidence that he was and, lacking such evidence, the likeness between them must be regarded as accidental — as springing from their community of interest, their common hatred of corrupt politics, their common yearning for the salvation of their beloved cities.

The interest of the Middle Ages in Aristophanes is attested by the manuscripts of his plays which have survived. The sands of Egypt have given up a few verses of the *Birds* written in the sixth century and a palimpsest fragment at Florence of the tenth century also contains a few verses of this play. In the eleventh century the great manuscript now at Ravenna was written. It alone of all the manuscripts in existence contains the entire eleven plays. With the plays in this manuscript are also included introductions and a full explanatory commentary. Mr. Rogers thinks it not impossible that this manuscript may be the actual transcript of Suidas and his pupils.

About a century later in some Byzantine monastery seven of the plays with notes were carefully copied. This manuscript is now one of the most treasured possessions of the Library of Saint Mark's in Venice. The four plays omitted were the *Acharnians* and the three "women plays," the *Lysistrata,* the *Ecclesiazusae* and the *Thesmophoriazusae.* Beginning with the thirteenth century the manuscripts are more common — there are about one hundred and seventy in all.[34]

As in later times, so too at Byzantium and during the Middle Ages, the *Plutus* was the most popular play. It is preserved in no less than one hundred and forty-eight manuscripts, and it occupies the first place in the Ravenna and the Venetian manuscripts. The second and third places in these manuscripts are occupied by the *Clouds* and the *Frogs* and these plays are preserved in one hundred and twenty-seven and seventy-six manuscripts respectively. The other plays did not gain so wide a popularity. There are only twenty-eight manuscripts of the *Knights,* eighteen of the *Birds,* fourteen of the *Acharnians,* ten of the *Wasps,* eight of the *Peace.* The "women plays" close the list. The *Lysistrata* occurs in only eight manuscripts, the *Ecclesiazusae* in seven and the *Thesmophoriazusae* in but two.

The survival of Aristophanes is therefore not due to any mere chance or the accidental whim of some scribe. It was a widespread and deserved popularity that has preserved to us his buoyant wit, his keen criticism and his clear poetry. The vagaries of chance have left much from the great *corpus* of ancient writers that could well be spared withal. There is much which would be given gladly for a single burning ode of Sappho or Cean dirge of Simonides. But in preserving Aristophanes the god of chance, by whatever name he most delights to be called, has been kind. Or was it, as Matthew Arnold says, the same instinct for self-preservation that saves the race? [35]

" He (Aristophanes), too, like Sophocles, regards the human nature of his time in its fullest development; the boldest creations of a riotous imagination are in Aristophanes, as has been justly said, based always upon the foundation of a serious thought; politics, education, social life, literature — all the great modes in which the human life of his day manifested itself — are the subject of his thoughts and of his penetrating comment. There is shed, therefore, over his poetry the charm, the vital freshness, which is felt when man and his relations are from any side adequately, and therefore genially, regarded. Here is the true difference between Aristophanes and Menander. A great English statesman is said to have declared that there was no lost work of antiquity which he so ardently desired to recover as a play of Menander. Yet Menander has perished, and Aristophanes has survived. And to what is this to be attributed? To the instinct of self-preservation in humanity. The human race has the strongest, the most invincible tendency to live, to develop itself. It retains, it clings to what fosters its life, what favors its development, the literature which exhibits it in its vigour; it rejects, it abandons what does not foster its development, the literature that exhibits it arrested and decayed. Now, between the times of Sophocles and Menander a check had befallen the development of Greece.

"It is Athens after this check, after this diminution of vitality, — it is man with part

of his life shorn away, refined and intelligent
indeed, but sceptical, frivolous, and dissolute,
— which the poetry of Menander represented.
The cultivated, the accomplished might ap-
plaud the dexterity, the perfection of the representation — might prefer it to the free genial
delineation of a more living time with which
they were no more in sympathy. But the instinct of humanity taught it, that in the one
poetry there was the seed of life, in the other
the seed of death; and it has rescued Aristophanes, while it has left Menander to his fate."

The printing of Latin authors began with
Cicero's *De Officiis* and *Paradoxa* in 1465, and
before the first Greek text came from the press
about 1478 most of the Latin classics were in
type. The *editio princeps* of Aristophanes appeared in 1498 from the famous Aldine Press.
Again it may be taken as a proof of his popularity that Aristophanes was one of the first
Greek authors to be printed. The only notable
poets who preceded him were Homer (1488),
Hesiod (ca. 1493), Euripides, four plays (ca.
1495), the Bucolic poets (1496) and Apol-
lonius of Rhodes (1496); the only writers of
prose were Isocrates (1493), Aristotle (1495–
98) and Lucian (1496).

The *editio princeps* was published by Aldo Pio Manuzio. Its editor was the Cretan, Marco Musuro. It was originally the intention to include seven plays only and " finis " (τέλος) had actually been printed before the *Peace* and the *Ecclesiazusae* were added. The edition lacked the *Lysistrata* and the *Thesmophoriazusae*. In 1515 the Giunta Family in Florence issued a second edition in two parts (usually bound together). The first part contained the nine plays already published and the second part the two other plays. For some reason these two plays were again omitted from the second " Junta " edition published under the editorship of Antonio Fracini in 1525 and from the first edition published outside Italy — the edition of Gormont issued at Paris in 1528. Cratander in 1532 included the entire eleven plays in his edition issued at Basel and all subsequent editions contain them.

Meanwhile Aristophanes' influence was being exerted on contemporary writers. About 1504 that mordant soul, Macchiavelli, composed a comedy called *Le Maschere* on the model of Aristophanes. Assumed names were used but the identity of the great ecclesiastics

and statesmen attacked was sufficiently evident. At least so it appeared to Guiliano de
Ricci who suppressed the piece because of its
bitter satire and because of its tendency to
" ascribe all human things to natural causes
or to fortune."

With the publication of the plays, the *Plutus*
at once began to attract the most interest.
Even before the Aldine edition appeared,
Leonardo Bruni had desired a Latin translation of this play. In 1501 at Parma a translation of the *Plutus* into Latin trimeters was
published by Franciscus Passius and a little
later a Latin version of the *Plutus* and the
Clouds was made by Coriolanus Martitanus,
Bishop of Cosenza. By 1550 there were at
least ten Latin versions and about 1530 Pedro
Simon Abril completed a Spanish translation.
In Germany Petrus Mosellanus published a
separate edition of the *Plutus* in 1517 and the
next year another appeared at Louvain from
the hand of Erasmus' friend, Thierry Martens.

The great Hans Sachs at Nuremberg in 1551
produced the " *Pluto* " (!), an Aristophanic
drama in five acts. He must have used a Latin
version (there was certainly no German translation at that time) and he must have treated

his original with extreme freedom, for in the dénouement of the play there appears a Jew reduced to the utmost depths of despair by the wholesome financial order which is introduced by the God of Wealth after the restoration of his eyesight.

Aristophanes was an author familiar to the great figures of the Reformation. Melanchthon published an edition of the *Clouds,* and the *Plutus.* Some ardent friend of the Protestants attacked Luther's bitter enemy, Bishop Eck, in truly Aristophanic style in a play called " The plucked Eck " (*Eckius Dedolatus*) in which the *Plutus* is quoted thirteen times, the *Frogs* four, the *Clouds* three. It contains a parody on the tragic style, resembling the opening scene of the *Ecclesiazusae,* and a fabulous journey, modeled on the flight of Trygaeus in the *Peace.* Another trace of Aristophanes' influence may be seen in the chorus — a feature which distinguishes it from all Latin comedies.

One of Melanchthon's pupils writing at Basel in 1532 gives Aristophanes a novel recommendation. He is a master of diction, but, as a teacher of the young, he should be read in order that the student may contrast his obscenities with the purity of the Christian practice. At Zürich, Zwingli composed the music for the choral interludes in Georg Binder's presentation of the *Plutus* in the original Greek.

In the Basel edition of Erasmus' grammar there is a *colloquium* satirizing the grand style, in which Cornelia sings a song on the emancipation of women which is almost a translation of Calonice's song in the *Lysistrata,* and the interruptions of Margareta are in their *double entente* quite like Aristophanes. Erasmus founded his theory of teaching on the " duplex copia rerum et verborum." Style must be cultivated through the reading and study of authors who themselves are masters of style and who by the charm of their diction and the interest of their subjects hold the attention of their readers. To his students he then recommends Lucian, Demosthenes and Herodotus, and the poets Aristophanes, Homer and Euripides. In thus selecting Aristophanes as a model of style the great humanist is at one with the great teacher, Quintilian.

Luther forbade limiting the production of Latin and Greek plays, for he thought they not only helped in imparting a correct knowl-

edge of Greek and Latin but gave a picture of
the life of the people portrayed. The influence of Aristotle is here seen. His dictum that
"Comedy aims at representing men as worse,
tragedy as better than in actual life" and
Aristophanes' definition of a good poet as a
poet who makes good citizens fixed the standard by which comedies were judged. As Syrus
in Terence's *Adelphi* teaches his fellow slaves
to polish the pans till they become mirrors
which may reflect a pattern of life, so the
comedies of Aristophanes, Plautus and Terence
were produced as a holy warning to the youth
of the Reformation, to teach them what sort
of vices they were to avoid. An order for the
production of comedies in schools in 1552
says: "Comedy is a mirror of human life
which brands its disgraceful acts with polished
wits." A rather odd use for a mirror it must
be confessed.

This emphasis on the plays of Aristophanes
as a moral warning led to an even larger popularity for the *Plutus* and a corresponding neg-
lect of the other plays. The spirit of the time
was fond of allegory and of themes which admitted of a general application. The personal
nature of Aristophanes' satire did not lend

itself readily to such treatment. The *Plutus,*
just because it lacks the vivid personal qualities which make the earlier plays so unique —
because it belongs to the Middle rather than
to the Old Comedy — could serve the reformers' purpose and become a *speculum vitae.*
Hence its enhanced popularity.

The Latin plays of the Renaissance show
distinctly the influence of the Old Comedy in
one thing — the addition of a chorus, which
the plays of Plautus and Terence lack. This
is true of a play like Birk's *Susanna* though it
is not strictly a comedy. In Georg Marco-
pedius' *Aluta* a double chorus is employed —
an idea evidently borrowed from the *Lysistrata.*

Nicodemus Frischlin, who occupied many
academic posts in Germany for brief periods,
published editions of several of Aristophanes'
plays with introductions and a Latin translation. He was much hindered in his activities
by his literary and professional enemies — so
he claimed. Now it was a faithless " famulus "
who thwarted his plans, now an "academicus
diabolus," now a recalcitrant printer. He defended Aristophanes against the attack of Plutarch — deprecating the tendency to praise

one poet only at the expense of another. He thought the *Frogs* an answer to the *Palamedes* of Euripides which he conceived was a lament for Socrates' death. The *Birds* he believed referred to the events of the Peloponnesian War and " Cloudcuckooborough " was Decelea. In his own Latin compositions Frischlin followed Aristophanes in his method of personal attack. He did, however, employ fictitious names for his enemies among whom Crisius held a conspicuous place. The *Julius Redivivus* is especially notable among his plays, because it once inspired the youthful Bismarck and because it is one of the first[36] modern dramas to contain passages in a foreign language. In the scene in Hades, Caesar and Cicero are compelled to listen to French and Italian. It is conceivable that this idea may have been taken from Plautus' *Poenulus,* but it is more natural to suppose that the author had in mind the foreign ambassadors in Aristophanes who always talk a barbarous jargon or poor Greek. In one respect these plays of Frischlin do not resemble Aristophanes. All but the *Phasma* lack the chorus. The fondness of the writers of this period for allegory is again instanced in Naogeorgius' *Pammachius.*

This play has many Aristophanic elements and introduces two allegorical characters, analogous to *Plutus*, *Veritas* and *Parrhesia*. The first German version of the *Clouds* — a paraphrase rather than a translation — appeared in connection with a performance of this comedy in Greek at the Academic Theater in Strassburg in 1613.

So marked, in fact, is the Aristophanic character of the literature of the Reformation in Germany that this is often called the " Aristophanic period " of German literature. The influence of the poet is not so conspicuous in individual works, though the preceding pages amply attest his direct influence at many points. It is rather that the whole humanistic movement was so filled with the life-giving sanity of his clear and cleansing wit that the classical writers instinctively made him their model. Much of the clarity and sanity of the great writers who fought the deadly apathy of the Catholic hierarchy and the venomous spite of the Inquisition was due to their familiarity with the wholesome laughter of the shrewd Athenian patriot.

VI. ARISTOPHANES' INFLUENCE ON GERMAN WRITERS

THROUGHOUT the eighteenth century in Germany the question which most interested students of Aristophanes was the poet's relation to Socrates. Was the *Clouds* an attack on Socrates personally? Or did Aristophanes think of him as a type? Was the play merely the outcome of a standing feud between philosophers and poets or were Socrates and Aristophanes personal enemies? How is it possible to reconcile the attitude of Socrates toward Aristophanes in the *Apology* with the relations existing between the two men in the *Symposium?* Did Socrates' character and interests change between the time the *Clouds* was written and his trial and execution? These questions were most actively and vindictively discussed. The *Clouds* was more popular than the *Plutus.* Both had been translated into German, but no complete translation of the poet's works appeared till 1821.

[116]

Moses Mendelssohn regarded the *Clouds* as the work of a really corrupt man. Palmer von Grentemesnil accepted the belief that there was a traditional feud between the writers of comedy and the philosophers. At the beginning of the eighteenth century Tychsen maintained that the tradition of the Old Comedy was one of personal attack and that, therefore, it was contrary to its nature to employ Socrates as a type of sophistical philosopher. The attack was personal, the character was an approximation to Aristophanes' idea of Socrates. Wieland, conceiving Aristophanes as a force hostile to virtue, agrees that the attack on him by Aristophanes was personal — otherwise Gorgias or one of the other well known sophists would have been the chief character in the *Clouds*. The portrait is personal but modified by humor — no personal harm was intended.

Lessing, though interested in poetry, found Aristophanes' comedies nothing but mere satire — scarcely worthy of consideration. If the characters are real people the comedy reverts to primitive poetry — a mere personal lampoon. Socrates is then nothing but a comedy-type, as Cato is a typical tragic hero. This is what Aristotle meant when he contrasted comedy and the lampoon, the former constructed on lines of probability with characteristic names; the latter an attack on individuals. This view of Lessing's would reduce the Old Comedy of Athens to a pale antecedent of the New Comedy. The eighteenth century literary critics no more understood Aristophanes than did Plutarch in the second century. Vives even elaborated a thesis that Aristophanes wrote his comedies when "filled with new wine " — a thesis which at least two other critics thought it worth their while to dispute.

Meanwhile with the period of "awakening " in German literature came some real attempts to imitate Aristophanes. Schlosser lamented that there was no drama like the Greek to purge the politics of his day, and in 1761 Hamann wrote a comedy entitled the *Clouds*. It had, however, in the first act little but the name in common with the Greek, while the second act was only a masquerade. Lenz's *Clouds* appears, however, to have contained more pungent material. The scene in which a local character ·was satirized under the name of Strepsiades was suppressed. Only a single scene survives. In this, Wieland appears, as Socrates himself, engaged in a comedy of seduction and employing the hairsplitting dialectic of the philosophical schools. Another fragment of Lenz's work is from a play in which Bacchus descends to Hades and there meets Faust.

Goethe was on the whole indifferent to Aristophanes and showed little real acquaintance with his comedies. The weird confusion which arises from the actions of Hercules in Goethe's *Götter, Helden und Wieland* is truly Aristophanic, though there is little if any direct influence. In the second act of the *Triumph of Sentimentality*, published four years later in 1777, there is an almost exact translation of part of Praxagora's opening speech in the *Ecclesiazusae*. *The Birds, after Aristophanes,* published the next year, is probably not a political document but has many contemporary allusions. "Hopeful" and "Truefriend" set forth on a journey to Utopia — a land where lunches, passions and literary men are all alike free. They are led by a great horned owl who flies away in disgust at this riotous living. A city in the air is founded after the fashion of the *Birds* with Epops Maximus Polycacaromerdicus as mayor. From this point on the play is a burlesque extravaganza not related to

the original. Here Goethe takes leave of
Aristophanes never to return to him again. In
the critique of the new humanism Aristophanes
has no part.

Gottfried Hermann and Friedrich August
Wolf, those two giants of classical erudition,
at the opening of the nineteenth century were
both interested in Aristophanes. Hermann
took no decided stand on the Aristophanes-
Socrates question but centered his attention on
the historical Socrates and those aspects of
his character which lent themselves to satire.
Wolf believed the portrait in the *Clouds* to be
a fairly accurate picture of Socrates as he was
when the play was written, for he was then
(thought Wolf) interested only in materialistic
speculation; the Socrates of Plato and Xenophon was in his opinion a later development.
It seems clear that Wolf is here trying to explain how Aristophanes could in the *Clouds*
have so bitterly attacked a man with whom he
later had such friendly relations as are pictured
in the *Symposium*. To what lengths critics
will go to explain this anomaly is shown by
the work of Reisig and Van Leuwen, both of
whom thought the satire of Socrates was intended for Euripides.

With the romantic movement in Germany came a better understanding of Aristophanes. This school of writers showed that the romantic irony was nothing but transcendental buffoonery — that New Comedy had arisen only after the comic genius of the people had exhausted itself. Tieck, the first writer of Aristophanic comedy in Germany, believed that a character must be reasonable to be funny and that therefore there must be some truth in Aristophanes' representation of Socrates. In the light of this fact he thought it necessary to correct the portrait drawn by Plato and Xenophon. His *Anti-Faust* is filled with satire and literary criticism. Aristophanes himself is introduced and Wieland, also. Tieck believed that Aristophanes not only satirized Socrates but also himself and his whole art in the speeches in which the poet in his own person addresses the audience. Roetscher, too, thought that every subject in comedy was handled with irony.

The interest of the Schlegel brothers in the drama is well known. They refused to limit themselves by applying to their comedies the canons of the classical authors. F. Schlegel was virulently attacked by Kotzebue in a satiric drama, the name of which at least has a modern ring, *The Hyperborean Ass or the Modern Education.* A. W. Schlegel thought that Aristophanes' antipathy to Socrates was partly personal and partly inspired by the ideals of Socrates' philosophy. Welcker saw in the attack merely a strife between the old order and the new. Heine had really great satiric powers, but his energies were largely spent in petty disputes, and there are only occasional vague reminiscences of Aristophanes in such works as, *Deutschland, Bäder von Lucca* and the attack on the political *Tendenzliteratur* contained in *Atta Troll.*

Hegel conceived Aristophanes as no mere buffoon but as one honestly opposed to the dialectic of Socrates and to the freedom and universality of the spirit. The actors in his comedies transport us into an atmosphere of subjective serenity. "The internal serenity and good humor of the character is never lost, no matter how riotous the ridicule. The calmness of soul which is the terminus of tragedy is the starting point of comedy and is temporarily lost only to be regained." [37] "Without reading Aristophanes it is impossible to conceive how blissfully happy men can be."

The Hegelian school began to interpret all the plays in this spirit of free subjectivity. Strepsiades represents the old order striving for new ideals (represented by Socrates) and always failing. The burning of the "Thinking Shop" is the triumph of the opposition. This type of interpretation continued till late in the nineteenth century. Steiner in 1899 thought that the idea of the *Birds* was to point out to a pitiable mankind that a God existed. Throughout this period little attention was paid to the "women comedies."

With all this discussion about the correctness of Aristophanes' view of Socrates it was evident that something had to be done in behalf of Euripides and Cleon. Droysen and Vischer (and Grote in England) came to Cleon's rescue. Mueller-Strubing also defends Cleon. He believed Aristophanes to be in league with the youthful aristocrats against the democracy, a conservative attitude which as Koch shows is characteristic of all Old Comedy but which may have been increased by the conservatism of the Archon and the Choregus whose coöperation was necessary before a play could be produced.

Platen's *Oedipus* and *Gabel* were undoubt-

edly influenced by Aristophanes. The latter
was a burlesque on the so-called "fate tragedy." One of the chief characters is a Jew.
The play has the Aristophanic features of a
chorus and a *parabasis*. The *Oedipus*, also a
parody, has some of the incidents of the *Frogs*.
It contains a play within the play. "Pub-
licum," like Dionysus, is seeking a good poet
— Nimmermann — whose friends Heine, Samen
Abrahams and others come in for their share
of the gibes. Laius, Oedipus and Jocasta all
appear in the inner play — the latter violently
embroiled with her court poets — a satire on
the Dresden *Liederkranz*. In this connection
it is interesting to note Grabbe's attack on this
coterie and on "Shakespeare and the Shakespeare Mania." In true Aristophanic style he
has introduced quotations and well-known
characters from the works of the authors attacked, such as *Maria Stuart* and *Wallenstein*.
There are several other plays by Platen which
show in their mythological allusions, their fan-
tasies, and their parodies reminiscences of
Aristophanes.

Political satire was not so highly developed;
for the governments of Germany would not
tolerate Aristophanic freedom of speech.

Rückert's *Napoleon* handles a theme, perfectly safe for a pamphleteer. It is a satire without chorus in which the characters appear under allegorical names. The *parabasis* is spoken by Napoleon and "Pantless" (*Ohnehosen*). Among the curiosities of invention may be mentioned the *Walls* (*Die Wände*) by Seeman and Dulk in which the chorus is composed of personified walls. One general characteristic of these political dramas is the fondness the authors evince for long compounded and hyphenated words — a desire easily satisfied by the idiosyncrasies of the German tongue. In many of them this is the most notable Aristophanic imitation. The best of these political dramas is *Die politische Wochenstube*, by Prutz, which appeared in 1845. This play has real Aristophanic quality. Effective use is made of the scene between Euripides and Dicaeopolis in the *Acharnians*. Richard Wagner's *Kapitulation* is not political, but is a satire on the French theater and on Victor Hugo.

In the battle between the philosophers and dramatists, whose relations have always been more close and vindictive in Germany than in England, it was inevitable that Aristophanic

material should be employed. So Gruppe in
his attack on Hegel has produced a comedy of
the Aristophanic type, which von Humboldt
and Boeckh thought a masterpiece. There is,
however, much more of the operatic element in
the chorus than in the original. In this comedy, *The Winds*, Hegel appears under the
pseudonym of "Absolutulus." The play has
much charm and as a heterogeneous extravaganza has few equals. One scene is laid in the
philosopher's study in Eutopia where a typical
argument about the negation of negation is in-
terrupted by the night wind, Nocturnus, who
carries off all the philosopher's papers. Other
winds take part in the riot and later Oberon's
horn is employed to display the pageant of
history. A Jew explains the method of making
his special liquor, a concrete spirit brewed on
a Hegelian recipe. One of his sons complains
of not having an absolute name and is in turn
whisked off to the ocean by Nocturnus. The
philosophers Kant, Fichte and Hegel, two
journalists and a cock fight add poignancy to
act three, at the close of which Hegel gives a
masked ball at the Café National in Berlin.
Here his pupils appear as birds. Nocturnus
again interferes, blowing the absolutist from

the absolute. All is confusion till Titania rescues the world.

Gruppe in this drama follows the lines laid down by Tieck, while Rosenkranz's *Center of Speculation* is derived from von Platen. The latter piece is composed in the Berlin dialect. A chorus of owls assembles at the news of Hegel's death — only one person is left who can understand Hegel and he misunderstands him. The foolish rivalry for the master's throne must now cease. The scene changes from Berlin to Vienna where the methodist, the orthodoxist and the neologist engage in a philosophic discussion over the merits of Schönbrunn and the band concert in the Prater. Absolute belief in Hegel, the Bible and Goethe is demanded by the orthodoxist. The choruses are rather detached songs — after the Euripidean fashion — in praise of various cities.

A third Hegelian drama is Heinrich Hoffmann's *Travelers on the Moon* (*Mondzügler*). It represents a successful attack by the philosophy of Hegel on the philosophy of Schelling. Squire Peter returns from wandering to the " dream city " where all is absolute philosophy. The subject for discussion is the "notion of

filth " (*Urbegriff des Drecks*). The relation
of this play to Aristophanes is perhaps more
direct than in the two other instances.

The anonymous *Birth of Helios,* a satire on
journalists, the police and the court, belongs to
this period as does also the *New Plutus* by
Neuberger published in 1862. The latter fur-
nishes an interesting variant on the *Plutus.*
"Count Have-nothing" and "Professor Know-
it-all" heal the god of his blindness, in spite
of the fact that they know that goodness is
only achieved through poverty. The consequent troubles of the newly-rich furnish the
laughter of the play. Even in theological
satire Aristophanes' influence can be traced in
Kyau's *Theological Complaints.*

A more remarkable reminiscence of Aristophanes is the *Frogs,* by an unknown author
who styles himself "Philander von Sittewald
der Jüngere." The Berlin theater-director, like
Dionysus, undertakes a journey to the nether
world to recover a great poet. The comic
stage is represented by well known contemporaries. Immermann is rejected as an un-
satisfactory poet because he is too hard, Holtei
because he is too tedious, Heine because he
is entirely political. At the Styx, a chorus of

Berlin journals in the guise of frogs is encountered. In Hades a dramatic contest similar to that in the *Frogs* of Aristophanes is held. Schiller (Aeschylus) strives against Raupach (Euripides), while Heinrich von Kleist is cast for Sophocles. Schiller explodes Raupach's verses with snuff as Aeschylus does Euripides' with " a wine skin lost." In the contest at the scales where the poet's words are weighed, Schiller is again triumphant and is taken back to Berlin. An excellent political satire, also based on the *Frogs,* was published in 1867 at Vienna by "Aristophanes of Prague." It was embellished with song and music much like later opera.

Perhaps the best imitation of Aristophanes was produced by Julius Richter, in three plays written in Greek. The style and meter are close imitations of Aristophanes. The plays are preceded by hypotheses written in the Alexandrian style. The first to appear was the *Insects* in 1871. The play opens with a dialogue between two students of philology who, as in Aristophanes, give the setting for the play which is a satire on contemporary philologues and schoolmasters — notably Moritz Haupt, Wolf and Lachmann. There is a visit to

Hades where Frau Reiske, a friend of Lessing's, and Madame Dacier meet the travelers and dance for their benefit a *cordax* — a dance that is modern in every particular. Charon has raised his fare to three obols — an advance of three hundred percent. In Hades the heroes of classical Greece are introduced, Pericles rejoicing over the new Olympian on earth, i.e. Otto von Bismarck. A lyric on the Rhine skillfully combines parodies on Pindar and the German university songs.

In 1873 the *Swallows*, or the ultra-montane communists, followed. This is an equally brilliant attack on two opposite tendencies in the society and politics of the day. Reaction is confronted with violent radicalism. The interest is enhanced by the parallels that could be easily drawn between the small Greek communities and the German states before the foundation of the Empire. In the lyrics at the close there are interesting reminiscences of *Die Wacht am Rhein*. The following year the *Cuckoos* appeared, an Aristophanic treatment of events in current history. These Greek imitations all have much of the real spirit of the original. The parallels in structure and meter are careful and accurate. The introduction of rhyme is one of the few departures from the ancient versification.

How much damage can be done by an unsound theory let loose among philologians is shown by Brentano's adaptation of F. A. Wolf's Homeric theory to the plays of Aristophanes. Brentano thought that the plays had been worked over by a redactor in Byzantium and that the present text represented the combination of the work of at least two separate dramatists! The *Plutus,* for instance, contains one very old theme, a social tendence-theme, the enriching of mankind by the god Plutus, and a second, much later, the enriching of all the good by the same god. Brentano was led to this fantastic interpretation by the loose connection between the first part of the play and the scenes that follow the *parabasis.* It remained for Zielinski [38] to emphasize the importance of the *agon* (the contest) and to demonstrate that this loose connection was the natural outcome of the origin and development of the Greek comedy.

Recently there have been produced in Germany three adaptations of the *Lysistrata:* the *Eternal Feminine (Das Ewig Weibliche)* by Robert Misch in Berlin in 1901 — a fantasy

introducing Lysander and the Amazons; Adolf
Wilbrandt's *Lady General,* 1892 — a free
adaptation of the *Lysistrata* and the *Ecclesiazusae;* and a vaudeville-operetta, the *Lysistrata,* by Paul Lincke in 1902. Josef Wid-
mann's *Maikäfer-komödie,* an insect comedy
satirizing the political conditions in Switzer-
land, is reminiscent of Aristophanes and has
attracted much attention.

Aristophanes' influence on the German
drama has been profound. He has touched
many writers of comedy both directly and indirectly. His comical devices and his phrases
have become the common stock in trade of the
modern writer of comedy. Reminiscences of
his wit ring out in the most unexpected places.
In Hauptmann's *Sunken Bell* we hear the
"Ko-ax" of Aristophanes' *Frogs.*

Just before the Great War began there
appeared a pamphlet, entitled, "Aristophanes,
a Mirror of our Times," showing that Aristophanes' influence as a critic of morals and
statecraft was still potent. The author, Professor A. B. Kneisel, aims to help in cleansing
the moral shame of the German folk who, in his
opinion, were suffering from the same deadly
tendencies that ruined the Greeks twenty-three

hundred years ago. Aristophanes fought these insidious maladies through his comedies; so that he may help to arouse again in Germany the spirit of 1813 the author translates in outline three plays: the *Knights*, an attack on radical democracy; the *Frogs*, an attack on materialism and rationalism; the *Clouds*, an attack on atheism. So again here in militant twentieth century Germany Aristophanes appears transcending the rôle of a mere writer of plays and the critic of literature and becomes the inspiring apostle of a finer national patriotism.

VII. ARISTOPHANES' INFLUENCE ON FRENCH WRITERS

ARISTOPHANES first appeared in France under the editorship of Gormont in 1528. This edition lacked the *Lysistrata* and the *Thesmophoriazusae*. No complete edition appeared in France till that of Wechel and Neobari in 1540 — eight years after Cratander's publication at Basel.

That pungent satirist, François Rabelais, had read many classic authors while his light was hid in a Franciscan convent in La Vendée and after his revolt and escape he read many more. He made Aristophanes his model and five of the Greek plays are either cited by name or quoted, the *Knights, Wasps, Clouds, Birds* and *Ecclesiazusae*. He may never have seen the *Lysistrata* and the *Thesmophoriazusae* — the latter would certainly have furnished him further material for advice on the subject of marriage given to Panurge in his third book. In the spirit of his satire Rabelais has reproduced much of the Aristophanic flavor — one of his contemporaries, Joachim duBellay, says he has made Aristophanes live again. Gargantua, the giant of Touraine, Pantagruel, his son, Panurge, the great adventurer, Friar John (whether he be a travesty on Cardinal Chatillon or Martin Luther or both) are all treated with an extravagant fantasy, especially in the third book, worthy of the Greek original. There is about them and their marvelous adventures a freshness, a spontaneity that is truly Greek. The ribaldry is worthy to be compared with that of the Old Comedy. Rabelais exhibits even at sixty-three an exuberance of spirit, a lack of all bitterness and morbidity that makes him really akin to his master. If we omit from Aristophanes all the glory of his poetry, the rare lyrics that " shine like a bird's white wing in the sunlight," the two satirists may fairly be compared. But this is to grant a great deal. Into the realm of real poetic inspiration and imagination Rabelais cannot penetrate. To that empyrean Aristophanes soars alone.

In 1549 Ronsard — the eldest of the seven French writers called the Pleiades — translated the *Plutus* into French and produced it at the college of Coqueret. The comedies written by this group of authors — the Pleiades — however owe little more than the name to Aristophanes. While pretending to follow his example they produced a set of plays that were little related to contemporary politics and art and that had little vogue beyond the confines of their select circle.

Pierre le Loyer in 1578 published his *Néphélococugie*, a very original adaptation of the *Clouds*. Obscenities are to be banished, special attention is to be given the chorus and all the actors are to speak " in character." His mystic character is seen in his handling of the chorus. The strophe is the movement of the heavens, east to west, the antistrophe the movement of the planets, west to east, the epode the repose of earth. To the text is prefaced an acrostic argument giving the title, " Les Cocus."

The scene is laid at Toulouse. The plot is very similar to that of the *Birds* but there are reminiscences also of Rabelais. The burlesque element is doubtless due to his influence. The two wanderers from Toulouse, Gerrin and Conrad, set forth to find. Cuckoo town. Gerrin denounces women in Aristophanic style and the pair find inspiration in a flask (Rabelais' " Oracle of the Bottle ") instead of a raven. Jean Cocus, half bird, half man (the counterpart of Tereus in Aristophanes) controls the action. Trouble arises over the worship of Priapus by the Cocus people. The choruses closely follow those of the *Birds* and there are songs imitating those of the Hoopoe and of the Nightingale. The Cocus is more ancient than the Gods. Two eggs were laid by Night — from one sprang Love, from the other the ancestors of Cocus who ruled Syria and Egypt. Later his power had waned. A city in the clouds is founded and an embargo laid on the sacrifices to the gods, as in the *Birds*. After the *parabasis,* a *commus* in praise of Cocus is spoken by the Quail. Many names are suggested for the new city, Paris, Poitiers, Bordeaux, Lyons. Finally " Néphélo-cocugie " is chosen. The close of the play presents an interesting variant on Aristophanes. Le Loyer proves himself a master of the black art too. An Astrologer comes to seek refuge in Néphélococugie. He replaces the oracle monger of the *Birds*. An Alchemist takes the place of the mathematician, Meton. Instead of the Police Commissioner an Aristotelian logician is introduced. No parallel is offered to

the Statute Seller. After a second *parabasis*
the city is divided into three classes, following
Plato's ideal state. Iris comes from heaven
and her presence has a mellowing effect on
the authorities. An embassy from earth an-
nounces the great benefits that are accruing to
men. Many wish to join the new state. A
criminal and a soldier appear. The latter
wishes to improve his valor by the possession
of wings. This is a satire on the uncouth mer-
cenaries of the time. An interesting specimen
of the thieves' dialect is introduced. The play
ends with a marriage song as in the original.
Here, as in the early German plays, the influence of Aristophanes is direct.

Seventeenth century France had little real
appreciation for Aristophanes. René Rapin
(1621–87) echoes Plutarch's criticism. To
him Aristophanes is low and vulgar. He
should be forbidden the theater. The ancient
comedy in his opinion pleased only the common people while Molière charmed the nobles
and all Paris. Terence is the ideal of the
literary critics, of Rapin and also of Nicolas
Boileau who thought that Aristophanes' comedies outraged good sense.

Racine's *Les Plaideurs* — his only venture in

comedy — is an adaptation of Aristophanes'
Wasps. But even here the author is most
apologetic; for in his preface he explains that
his play is not a real comedy such as Terence or
Menander would have written but an experi-
ment to see if the works of the Athenian playwright could be put on a modern stage. It
was first acted in the Hôtel de Bourgogne in
1668 and was not received with enthusiasm.
Racine felt that the taste of the audience compelled him to inject a love intrigue, and the
affair of Léandre and Isabelle makes a curious
combination with the madness of the old man.
Dandin is smitten with a craze for attending
court, as Philocleon in the *Wasps*. Petit Jean,
the portier, corresponds to Xanthias; Cicero's
speech for Quinctius, Aristotle, Pausanias and
the Digest are all quoted in the course of the
play. The old man appears through a hole
in the roof in true Aristophanic fashion, and a
dog is brought to trial as in the *Wasps*. There
are also a few parodies of lines in *Le Cid*. The
play closes naturally with the marriage of
Léandre and Isabelle.

One would like to think that Molière, so
close a student of Plautus and Terence, also
owed something to Aristophanes, and it has

been suggested that Strepsiades in the *Clouds* is the original of the *Bourgeois Gentilhomme*. In form there is often a correspondence. To take but a single instance, the scene of the *Amour Médecin,* one of the mask comedies, is laid in the open air before the house of Sganarelle. The three acts of the play as originally written were separated by interludes of dance and song. In this play too there was a further likeness to the work of Aristophanes, for the four doctors who are held up to ridicule were the four leading physicians of the court of Louis XIV, easily recognizable to the theatergoers of Paris. The attack upon contemporary persons is of the old Greek Comedy, but the scene where these four doctors violently disagree over the case submitted to them was probably suggested by the disagreement among the lawyers in Terence's *Phormio.* That Molière frequently satirized persons under the transparent veil of a pseudonym, as the Duc de Montausier who serves as the model for his *Misanthrope,* is well known. In spirit he is the direct descendant of Aristophanes. While the vices he attacks are usually social, not political, he does not hestitate to point his morals with a personal application, quite Aristophanic.

He has all of the Greek dramatist's freshness
and wit, he has the same freedom from morbidity and bitterness, the same wistful pity that
sometimes whispers from Aristophanes' lines
like a half smothered sigh.

> O *grudge not the youth their enjoyment*
> For *beauty the softest and best*
> Is *breathed o'er the limbs of a maiden*
> And *blooms on a maidenly breast.*[39]

"Who's for the rest from pain and sorrow?
Who's for the plains of the River of Forgetful-
ness?"[40] Molière's models were the poets of
the New Comedy undoubtedly. His comedies
are the descendants of Plautus and Terence,
but especially in such plays as *Tartufe* and
Festin de Pierre it is impossible to doubt that
in their deeper purpose they are critiques of
his time as Aristophanes' plays were of his.

It was with a realization of this fact that, in
celebrating the two hundred and seventy-fifth
anniversary of Molière's birth, January 15,
1897, the Comédie Française presented a short
play in verse by Jean Bertheroy — *Aristophanes et Molière.*

The shades of Molière and Aristophanes
look down on modern Paris. Molière is sur-

prised at the size of the modern city; Aristophanes, bewildered by the new world, at first thinks himself still in Greece. He is represented as pessimistic over the development of the human race. To Molière he says: " You were without doubt a censor as I, scourging in turn, the gods, man, and the law." Molière is more hopeful of man's ability to achieve a useful and peaceful destiny.

MOLIÈRE: *Through brotherhood the people have grown.*

ARISTOPHANES: *Yes, but common sense is everywhere benumbed.*

MOLIÈRE: *One sees fewer impostors. Speech is more frank.*

ARISTOPHANES: *And the number of fools multiplies in a torrent.*

MOLIÈRE: *A single true God has replaced your gods.*

ARISTOPHANES: *And when there were false gods, they were more loved.*

Aristophanes withdraws " to the clouds whither the souls of plants and waters are wafted. There the heaven becomes a rainbow and the birds soar." Humanity appears to Molière, to reassure him: " The past remains shaded. The present is still full of shadow. But look at the Dawn. The future shines there. The human race celebrates there the joy of your perfect work, keep your supreme faith, your fair, charming humor. I love you as you have loved me."

Among the Frenchmen of the seventeenth or eighteenth century who were lovers of the classics, Fénelon is conspicuous. Yet in a letter to Madame Dacier he could write: " I say that the amusing features of Aristophanes appear to me often bad, they constitute the farce made purposely to amuse and influence the crowd." He would, indeed, have been quite willing to discard Aristophanes altogether. His correspondent, Madame Dacier, however, was one of the very few to whom that course would not have been acceptable — she was one of the few who did the poet justice. Her father, Tanaquil Lefèvre, was a Greek scholar and teacher. He published an edition of the *Ecclesiazusae* with notes that prove him to have been no mere pedant. His son Tanaquil Junior saw fit to attack his father's conception of the ancient poets and especially his estimate of Aristophanes. The comedians, he said, attack decent people for the sole purpose of raising a laugh, and on the hill of Parnassus

[143]

Aristophanes is conspicuous as the murderer of Socrates. His sister, Madame Dacier, inherited her father's love for the Greek poets. She began an edition of the *Odyssey*. She wrote on the causes of the decay of taste and stoutly upheld the primacy of the ancient over the modern literature. She was devoted to Aristophanes. It is said that she had read the *Clouds* two hundred times before she attempted to translate it. She produced also her translation of the *Plutus,* preserving the unity of time by giving the first two acts in the evening and the last three the next morning. She complains that in her time the influential people attended the performance of comedies only that they might witness a love intrigue — only to satisfy their morbid passions. Aristophanes' plays far transcended such disgraceful scenes: " He has found the means to make natural the things farthest from his subject and of making his caprices and conceits seem the natural result of preceding events." She contributed much to the appreciation of Aristophanes, her translations are frequently cited and her name is often coupled with that of the poet whom she alone justly esteemed.

The attitude of eighteenth century France

was no more friendly toward Aristophanes. The comedy of manners was still the ideal and Terence and Molière supreme. Bernard le Bovier de Fontenelle, who wrote dialogues of the dead after the fashion of Lucian, apposing men of different ages as Socrates and Montaigne, disparaged all Greek writers in comparison with the Romans. He was especially bitter toward the tragedians. Aristophanes, he admits, has some excellent scenes. The sophists, not Socrates, are the object of attack in the *Clouds* and Strepsiades is the prototype of the " Bourgeois Gentilhomme." This tendency to make the comedy of manners the standard, even to interpret the work of Aristophanes in its terms may be seen more clearly in Pierre Bayle's *Dictionnaire Historique et Critique*. It contains no article on Aristophanes, but criticises him because he is too much bound by conventions of time and place, that is, his comedies are local and not universal as is the New Comedy. This is even more clearly stated in Brumoy's *Théâtre des Grecs* (1730). Here it is revealed that the *Clouds* is really a school for all fathers. The moral which the *Wasps* teaches is that the liberty to follow first impulses is slavery but that not to follow them leads to even greater slavery. The purpose of the *Frogs* is to point out the folly of the Athenians in extending the franchise to slaves and aliens. To Brumoy, Aristophanes is a plain moralist; to Goguet he is the one character that spoils fifth century Athens; to Chamfort he is merely the buffoon of the people. Boivin has nothing better to say of the *Birds* than that it is bizarre, catering to the corrupt customs of the Athenians and debasing their ideas of the gods. La Harpe finds Aristophanes no comedian and at most merely a satirist. He is at a loss to see how he could have produced the *Knights*. He condemns the *Wasps* and the *Clouds* for their lack of intrigue, of plot, of character drawing.

There were not lacking, it is true, a few sound critics who defended Aristophanes. Fréron says that tragedy corrects passion through fear, and comedy reforms vice through ridicule. To present the serious in a pleasant way was an art possessed by Aristophanes and Molière alone. Aristophanes has made comedy an organ of patriotism; he has not the real spirit of true comedy. Pierre-Charles Lévesque represents a notable advance in French criticism. He reproaches the critics because they blame Homer for not reproducing modern customs and Aristophanes for pleasing the Athenian audience and not the courts of Louis XIV and Louis XV. He notes the difference between the ancient and modern audiences — that a play in Greece did not have to appeal to a large general public but only to the immediate spectators. He straightforwardly attacks Plutarch for his defamation of Aristophanes. Palissot also disagrees with the commonly accepted estimate of Aristophanes. It is the great merit of his comedies, he says, that the characters are so well drawn, that in spite of all the exaggeration made necessary by theatrical production, the truthfulness of Aristophanes' representations is not obscured. No change of time or place can obscure that. Aristophanes is still to him the model and to be called by his name is an admission that the author has reached his goal. In his comedy, *The Philosophers*, much Aristophanic material is observable. Rousseau and the Encyclopedists are treated to much the same ridicule that the sophists and Socrates suffered in the *Clouds*.

But of all Aristophanes' critics perhaps Voltaire is the most severe. It seems scarcely credible that he should have so misjudged any

literary production. One of his contemporaries says that Voltaire treated Aristophanes as
if he were an immature French poet attacking
the French philosophy of his own day. In
fact Voltaire says that he is a comic poet, who
is neither a writer of comedy, nor a poet. He
would not be allowed to produce his plays at
the " foire Saint-Laurent." He is even worse
than Plutarch thought him and he it was who
prepared the poison with which the infamous
judges were to kill the most virtuous man in
Greece.

Madame de Staël apparently did not know
Aristophanes at first hand. But to her as to
most of her contemporaries Menander and his
comedy of manners is supreme. She believed
that the subordinate part played by women in
Greek affairs necessarily deprived them of
finesse and good taste. Interest is measured
by the rôle which women play. Judged even
by this feminine standard one would think
Aristophanes might have been " by merit raised
to that bad eminence."

There are so many elusive, ephemeral elements in Aristophanes' poems that they can
never be made the models for contemporary
drama. They have not the universality of the

New Comedy and since by their very nature
they were in this way unadaptable, most
French critics of the seventeenth and eighteenth centuries failed to perceive their supreme
merit. The influence of Cartesianism was still
too strong. Historical literary criticism had
not yet come into its own and in the contrast
between ancient and modern ideals Aristophanes inevitably suffered eclipse.

It would be interesting but unprofitable to
try to find Aristophanic influence in the vol-
umes of Chateaubriand. His works mark the
transition from the classical to the romantic
school. He is a brilliant writer of political
invective but nowhere does he show that he
has profited by studying the great Athenian
master of political satire.

The literary models of the seventeenth or
eighteenth centuries in France had been the
classics. The French Revolution sweeping
away traditions of every sort brought in the
Romantic Movement. The publication in
1824 of Victor Hugo's *Cromwell*, the production of Dumas' *Henri III* in 1829 and of
Hugo's *Hernani* in 1830 meant a complete
break with the classical drama. In Dumas
and Hugo one looks in vain for traces of the

Greek dramatist, but in Eugene Scribe's first successful play, *Une Nuit de la Garde Nationale,* a one-act vaudeville piece, there is a return to the Aristophanic practice of biting contemporary satire. In fact, Scribe's development of the vaudeville from a brief parody or anecdote to a play with a complete plot has many analogies to Aristophanes' ennobling influence on the Greek comedy. In his *Bertrand et Raton,* Bertrand is clearly an impersonation of Talleyrand. It is impossible not to think of the situation often arising in fifth century Athens, when it is remembered that Talleyrand himself attended the first performance of this play in London and applauded his double across the footlights.

One is tempted by such statements as the following of Dumas *fils* to speculate on the possibility of a serious classical influence: " We are lost unless we hasten to place this great art (the drama) in the service of important social reform and the high hopes of the soul. . . . Let us inaugurate, therefore, the useful theatre at the risk of hearing an outcry from the apostles of art for art, three words absolutely devoid of meaning." This looks very much like a revolt from the standard of individual judgment in literature and art which the Romantic movement inaugurated. But when the plays of Dumas are read it is quickly seen that they show no consistent moral purpose, no real relation to Aristophanes.

Émile Augier, however, in *Fils de Giboyer,* by boldly attacking the Clericals and the Jesuits for their intrigues in politics, won for himself the title of " the French Aristophanes." He was bitterly reviled by the press for his attack on the church and he was reminded that Aristophanes by his caricature of Socrates had brought about the death of the noblest man of his generation. Augier admitted that one of his characters, Deodat, had been drawn from contemporary Paris but instead of abandoning his theme to please his critics he produced two new plays, *Contagion* and *Effrontes,* on the same general subject, and a third, *Lions et Renards,* in which he reintroduced a character, St. Agathe, from *Fils de Giboyer.* While these plays resembled the work of Aristophanes in directness and while it would be interesting to imagine that Augier pursued St. Agathe through a series of plays as Aristophanes pursued Cleon, it must be confessed that these plays have no resemblance to the *Clouds* and the *Knights* in their plot or structure. The author owes nothing to Aristophanes except the inspiration of a courageous example.

Victorien Sardou, however, in his deliberate attacks on republicanism in his *Oncle Sam,* a satire on American government, and in his more brilliant and ruthless attack on Gambetta, in *Rabagas,* is deliberately following Aristophanes. Not that he tries to adapt the scenes of the Greek plays to his comedies, but it is clear in many an allusion and many a telling thrust that he is trying consciously to follow the Athenian poet in his rôle as a political dramatist. Among the characters of *Rabagas,* Garibaldi is to be recognized. This excursion of Sardou into the political field was not well received. In fact when he was finally admitted to the Academy in 1878 he was publicly warned by Charles Blanc that these political satires were not always well conceived nor suited to his talents. In spite of this, the following year he produced as his first work as an academician, *Daniel Rochat* — an attack on the Church and especially on its priests. This too failed dismally at the Comédie Française.

In later years there have been at Paris some

interesting revivals of Aristophanes' plays. In 1892 Maurice Donnay revived the *Lysistrata*. In this he replaced many of the references to Athenian and Spartan women by references to modern Parisiennes and Parisian customs but the play was in all its essentials as Aristophanes wrote it and its production caused comment even in Paris. In 1896 Paul Gavault, the author of *The Belle of New York* and other light plays, successfully produced the *Plutus*, and in 1911 Fernand Nozières adapted the *Birds* to the Paris stage.

Rostand's *Chantecler*[41] was also hailed as a revival of Aristophanes' *Birds*, but it is not, except in the whimsical character of some of its conceits and the bare externals of the costumes. It is a lineal descendant of Chaucer's *Chanticleer*. For in both of these the dramatist is interested in the activities of the fowls themselves. The barnyard has become for the nonce an actual world peopled with feathered personalities. "Aristophanes," as Rostand himself says, "made use of his birds to criticize the follies of his contemporaries. My piece employs satire only by the way." The *Insect Play* by the Capek brothers, recently produced (fall of 1922) in New York, which satirized the vanities and passions of mankind by showing the results of these passions as displayed in their crude essentials in the lives of insects, is much more in Aristophanes' vein than *Chantecler*.

There is much modern French drama that has the spirit of Aristophanes' keen criticism, there are flashes that recall his wayward imagery and his exuberant imagination. Hugo has almost his lyric charm but nowhere is there a dramatist who combines these elements so that he is worthy to receive the great Comedian's mantle — few who can be surely said to have harkened to his message.

VIII. ARISTOPHANES' INFLUENCE ON ENGLISH WRITERS

THE *Plutus* is, of all Aristophanes' comedies, the most susceptible of imitation because it deals, not with individuals, but with the vicissitudes of fortune to which humanity in general is subject. To understand it the audience needed no erudite knowledge of fourth century Athens but only an acquaintance with those ills to which all flesh is heir. As might have been expected, then, it was the earliest of Aristophanes' comedies to be produced in England. It was also the most popular. A tradition says that it was acted in Greek before Queen Elizabeth.   It certainly was acted at Cambridge in 1536 where ten years later the *Peace* was produced.   The first English translation of the *Plutus* was made in 1651 and several others followed in the next seventy years.

Aristophanes had a profound influence on the classical plays given at the universities and on the *Soties,* farces produced by the " Enfants

sans Souci " of Paris to which the morality
plays in England were indebted. Among the
more popular of the former were *Club Law,
Pedantius* and the *Parnassus Trilogy*. This
trilogy contained caustic comments on the
popular stage and a parody of the examination
inflicted on Strepsiades in the *Clouds*. *The
Ignoramus,* by Ruggle, first produced at Trinity
College, Cambridge, on the occasion of the visit
of King James I and Prince Charles in 1615,
far surpassed the others in brilliance and wit.
It was an attack by the wearers of the gown
on the townsmen and especially on the
unpopular recorder, Brackyn. Ignoramus
talks a hodgepodge of bad Latin and legal
terms. The humiliating and extravagant adventures through which he goes, culminating in
an unexpected marriage with the wrong girl
and incarceration in a monastery, are drawn
largely from Italian comedies.

There is little trace of Aristophanes' influence on the English drama before 1600.
Parallels pointed out in Udall's *Ralph Royster
Doyster* seem entirely fanciful, and very little
connection can be shown between the *Plutus*
and *All for Money* by Lupton Thomas (1578).
In *Foure Letters Confuted* Thomas Nashe

(1592) showed apparently a more just appreciation of Aristophanes' merits than was current among the critics for many a day. " Thee I embrace, Aristophanes, not so much for thy Comoedie of the cloud, which thou wrotst against philosophers, as for in al other thy inuentions thou interfusest delight with reprehension." Tomkis' *Albumazar* (1614) and *Lingua,* a comedy produced about the same time, both have references to the *Clouds.*[42] But, on the whole, sixteenth century England found Virgil superior to Homer, and Plautus to Aristophanes.

Ben Jonson is of all English dramatists the one most influenced by " tart Aristophanes." His lyrics sometimes show an Aristophanic vigor and wealth of fancy, as the song of Cock Lorrel in the *Masque of the Metamorphos'd Gypsies.* In the *King's Entertainment* Plutus and Peace appear. Plutus is not old and blind, as in the Greek play, but a charming youth, and Peace is the bride of Trygaeus, the giver of grapes.

In the *Poetaster* (1601) he adopts Aristophanes' method of literary-political satire. The Poetaster follows the *Frogs* in general outline but there is no close correspondence in

details. The *personae* of the drama are
Augustus Caesar and his court. Among them
are Horace, Ovid, Virgil, Maecenas, Tucca,
Crispinus and others. That most of these
characters represented contemporaries of Jonson is unquestioned. Most of them can not
now be identified with certainty. Horace is
Jonson himself; Crispinus is John Marston,
Demetrius is Thomas Decker, Virgil may be
Shakespeare or Chapman. The trial of the
Poetaster which occurs in the fifth act has no
resemblance to the trial in the *Frogs*. The
idea only is Aristophanic. There is nothing
of the scope and universality of the Greek
criticism — and little of its rare wit. In the
end Virgil pronounces judgment; Horace is
justified, Crispinus is given an overdose of
physic and Demetrius is arrayed as the court
fool.

The *Epicoene or the Silent Women* is a free
adaptation of the *Plutus,* and there are also
slight reminiscences of Aristophanes in *Bar-
tholomew Fair,* and in *Volpone* the motive
of the " Magnetic Lady " is Aristophanic.
Socrates measuring the feet of the fleas in the
Clouds is alluded to in *Timber* and this same
incident is again referred to in *The Devil is an*

Ass (1616) where Pug, the little devil, prays
to his master devil that he may rather

> Keep *fleas within a circle, and be accomptant*
> A *thousand years, which of them and how far*
> Out *leaped the other, than endure a minute*
> Such *as I have within.*

In the preface to *Every Man out of his
Humor* Jonson discusses the character of the
Old Comedy and Comedy in general.   He
comes continually back to Cicero's definition:
" an imitation of life, a mirror of custom, a
picture of truth."   His attitude toward his own
comedy is quite like that of Aristophanes in
some of his *parabases*.   In the introduction to
Every Man out of his Humor he says:

> I *fear no mood stamp'd on a private brow*
> When *I am pleased t' unmask a public vice,*
> I *fear no strumpet's drugs, no ruffian's stab*
> Should *I detect their hateful luxuries,*
> No *broker's, usurer's or lawyer's gripe,*
> Were *I disposed to say, they are all corrupt.*
> I *fear no courtier's frown should I applaud*
> The *easy flexture of his supple hams.*

From other references it is clear that Jonson
was not only familiar with the plays of Aristo-

phanes but that he had also read the scholia on them.

In *Cynthia's Revels* (1600) Jonson had introduced Lady Argurion, a possible antecedent to Lady Pecunia, Infanta of the Mines, who is one of the leading characters in the *Staple of News*. The latter appeared in 1625 and owes much to the *Plutus* and the *Wasps*, though the whole situation is treated with a deal of originality and freedom. Penni-Boy speaks to Lady Pecunia in Act II, scene 1, in much the strain adopted by Chremylus to Plutus, and Blepsidemus' eagerness to see Plutus has its counterpart in Pyed Mantle's desire to meet Lady Pecunia. In Act IV, scene 3, parts of the debate between Penni-Boy, Uncle Penni-Boy and Lady Pecunia seem almost a translation of the Greek. The trial of the dogs in Act V, scene 4, was probably suggested by the similar scene in the *Wasps*. The addition of such allegorical figures as Wax, Mortgage and Bond is due to Jonson's own fertile imagination.

Jonson was a poet of the most robust humor. He was fond of bringing together scenes from his own experience and combining them with airy creations of his bold imagination. In all this he was a worthy follower of his Greek master. The lyrics in his dramas, however, are cast in the Horatian mould and lack the laughing spontaneity, the swift upborne flight of Aristophanes' pure poetry.

In 1651 *Hey for Honesty; down with Knavery* was brought out by " F. J." in London. The most probable solution for " F. J.'s " identity is Thomas Randolph. The play purports to be a translation of the *Plutus,* but is really an original conception with only the details of the Aristophanic play. Aristophanes himself appears in the prologue. The oracle at Delphi is consulted and its advice leads to the discovery of Plutus. He inaugurates an ideal reign in which Poverty is banished, righteousness exalted and the guilty, including Hunger, are punished. Most of the fun in the play is in the dialect employed by Clodpole, Lackland, Scrape-all, and Dullpate. Latinized forms like " Godamercatus " enliven the conversation. A new figure, Pastor Dikaeus, replaces Chremylus of the original. He prays that he may forget all his Latin and Greek. Rev. Cliplatin lives a riotous life on £20 per annum granted him by his college. Poverty summons her forces for a battle. The Irish and Scotch come to the aid of the English with a vast medley of dialects. A song adapted from Aeschylus is sung by one of the priests. Mercury trying to avoid the consequences of his lies " by a metaphore " is reminiscent of the apology given by Dionysus to Euripides for breaking his promise (a quotation from one of Euripides' own plays) — " the tongue swore," etc. The Pope, " Jupiter's Vicar," appears and is roughly handled, being left to starve when all the rest but Dullpate are enriched by Plutus. Randolph's play is an elaboration of the *Plutus* and is also a more stringent satire on contemporary morals than is the original. The attack on the Church is especially bitter. Randolph, like Jonson, believed in the moral message of his plays and both believed that this could be best conveyed through the Aristophanic form.

Thomas Carew in *Coelum Britannicum,* a masque performed at Whitehall in 1633, uses Aristophanic material in his treatment of Plutus and Penia. The power of wealth even among the gods is admitted by Jupiter, who woos Danaë in a shower of gold. H. H. Bornell in 1659 also made a free adaptation of the *Plutus* under the caption, *The World's Idol or Plutus, the God of Wealth.*

Beaumont and Fletcher in *Four Plays* or *Moral Representations* make use of characters from the *Plutus*, and in the *Woman's Prize or the Tamer Tamed* they freely adapt the *Lysistrata* with some reminiscences of the *Ecclesiazusae*. In both the English and the Greek plays the women revolt against the men and bring them to terms by secession. The women are led by Base Biancha — a parallel to Lysistrata — and the men by Petruchio, a woman tamer. Women of town and country appear in the *Tamer Tamed* as Athenian and Spartan women take part in the Greek original. The outrageous English used by Maria corresponds to the broad Doric of Lampito. In both plays the men are put to flight by a chorus of women. The oath by which the women, English and Athenian, bind themselves to live apart from their husbands is identical; and in each case the men are brought to terms because they cannot endure the separation. The English play is not so coarse as the Greek and there is more interest in the study of female character.

The *Ecclesiazusae* furnished the idea of a women's state which Cartwright used in his *Lady Errant*. The scene is laid in Cyprus and

the women secure control of the state by seiz-
ing the treasury.

Indirectly, through the *Tamer Tamed*,
Aristophanes furnished Shakespeare the theme
which he treated in his *Taming of the Shrew*.
There is no obvious connection between Aristophanes and Shakespeare but there are a few
passages in the *Timon* which have Aristophanic
parallels; Aristophanes' lost play, *Timon*, may
have furnished through Plutarch and Lucian
some of the material for Shakespeare's play.
But to deduce from these doubtful parallels
any relation between the world's two greatest
masters of comedy is purely fanciful. Their
connection with each other lies far beyond the
reach of the critic's probe in that well of
" laughter which is a sudden glory."

There are reminiscences of Aristophanes in
Massinger's *A City Madam* (1659) and in
Middleton's *The Old Law*. But the latter's
Game of Chess (1623) is, if Swinburne's opin-
ion be adopted, " the only work in English
poetry which may properly be called Aristo-
phanic." It is a bitter attack on the Catholic
Church and on the Spaniards. The "Game "
is between two prelates, one of the Church of
England, the other of the Catholic Church.

King James is introduced into the play. The hatred of the Spaniards was at the time intensified by the war in the Netherlands. So bitter was the feeling aroused by this political satire that the play was suppressed at the instance of the Spanish ambassador.

The writers of the following period saw little in Aristophanes to interest them. Jeremy Collier (1698), expressing himself concisely in his " Short View of the Immorality and Profaneness of the English Stage," calls Aristophanes "A downright atheist," and William D'Avenant looks on him with only a slightly milder disfavor. It seems probable that Farquhar (1678–1707) derived " Aimwell " and " Archer " in his *Beaux Stratagem* from Euelpides and Peisthetaerus in the *Birds*.

Samuel Foote (1720–1777), who had been an Oxford student and who was familiar with the classics, is sometimes called " the Aristophanes of the English stage." He is like Aristophanes neither in insight nor fancy nor poetic genius nor in the freedom of his art. But he does resemble the Greek poet in this: the persons who appear on his stage are contemporary characters, though the names are disguised — as Aristophanes himself converts

Cleon into the Paphlagonian. On occasion, too, the identity of the characters is disclosed, and it must have been patent often to the listening audience. Beginning with a sort of vaudeville monologue, Foote built his comedies gradually into semi-serious criticism of individuals and customs. This gave him a considerable vogue and must have lent to his performances something of the personal spice which an Athenian audience found in Aristophanes.

Among later plays derived directly from Aristophanes, Shelley's *Swellfoot, the Tyrant* is remarkable. The play was taken, as he said, " from a Doric original." Various animals are given parts and the chorus is composed of swine. In one of the choral odes the pigs celebrate their genesis as do the *Birds* in their great *parabasis*. They utter their " characteristic note " as do the *Frogs*. Swellfoot and his queen, Iona Taurina, are none other than George IV and Queen Caroline and the ministers Purganax, Dakry and Laoctonos are Lord Castlereagh, Lord Eldon and the Duke of Wellington. No wonder the play was at once suppressed and was not included with Shelley's published works for many years.

In 1852 there appeared at Oxford, " Scenes from an unfinished Drama " entitled "*Phron-tisterion or Oxford in the 19th century,*" by Henry L. Mansel, afterward Dean of St. Paul's. It is a remarkably close adaptation of certain scenes in the *Clouds,* a satire on the German philosophers and on the academic reforms attempted by Lord John Russell's University Commission. *The Cambridge Dionysia,* a *Classic Drama* written by George Otto Trevelyan in 1858, is a brilliant adaptation of the *Wasps,* and his *Ladies in Parliament,* written on the occasion of the rejection of Gladstone's reform bill in 1866, was " at first intended to be a modern and decent *Ecclesiazusae.*" And though it does not follow the Greek with any accuracy or in any detail it has much of the spirit of the Old Comedy in the wit of its contemporary allusions.

It has been remarked that the nearest analogy to Aristophanes' comedies is the light opera. And of all the writers of light opera in England Sir William Gilbert is by far the one best entitled to don the mantle of Aristophanes. In fact he was given the title of "the English Aristophanes " in a recent appreciation.[43] His fancy plays lightly about some of the Aristophanic conceptions. His land between heaven and earth is the " Cloudcuckooborough " of the *Birds*. The theme of the *Lysistrata* is used in *The Princess,* and the English Parliament is the object of his delicate political ridicule in the *Peer and the Peri*. His world, like that of Aristophanes, " is not one of nonsense but one of sense upside down." His plays have more dramatic unity than do the Greek plays. His characters are carefully drawn — they are not caricatures — and his satire is only lightly ironical. He lacks the fiery earnestness, the vivid hatreds, the moral passion of Aristophanes.[44]

It is not necessary to mention here the recent revivals of Aristophanes. In spite of the great interval of time and space that separates the modern world from fifth century Athens, in spite of the many allusions that escape us, his plays still charm whether they are given in Athens or Munich or Oxford or Berkeley.[45]

That Aristophanes should have been the delight of classical students is not strange. But his circle of influence is much wider. He is the friend not only of dramatists but of all literary folk. In the statutes for the founding of Caius College in 1572 a hardened offender

is said to be like the Spartans in the *Acharnians*
with whom,

> " *no engagement sacred stands,*
> N*ot the altar, not the oath pledge, not the faith of*
> *clasped right hands.*"

Robert Burton in his *Anatomy of Melancholy*
displays a thorough acquaintance with the poet,
quoting from several of his plays. He compares a love melancholy to the plight of the
men in the *Lysistrata* and in the cure for love
melancholy he again quotes the same play:
"an old man may marry but a girl's season is
short." Spenser and Milton speak of Aristophanes, the latter, it must be confessed, with
sorrow. To Swift (of all men!) he "too
vicious and profane is," though Swift probably
owes his " Floating Island," where mathema-
ticians and philosophers dwell, to the " Thinking Shop" of the *Clouds*. Henry Cromwell
compared Pope's bitter satire to Aristophanes
and Pope returned the compliment by saying
that Cromwell was more like Cato the Censor
than he was like Aristophanes. Addison draws
the allegory which closes one of the papers in
the *Spectator* from the *Plutus*, and Macaulay,
whose critical faculty was seldom at fault,

writes of "the splendor and the grotesque
fairyland of the Old Comedy, rich with such
gorgeous hues, peopled with such fantastic
shapes and vocal alternately with the sweetest
peals of music and the loudest bursts of elfish
laughter."

One of the stanzas in *Poor Matthias*, a late
poem by Matthew Arnold, was evidently suggested by the noble *parabasis* in the *Birds*. It
begins:

> Was it as the Grecian sings,
> Birds were born the first of things,
> Before the sun, before the wind,
> Before the Gods, before mankind,
> Airy, ante-mundane throng —
> Witness their unworldly song!

Browning,[46] translator of Aeschylus and
careful student of the classics as he was, displays more familiarity with Aristophanes than
with any other Greek author. In *Aristophanes' Apology* he not only shows that he has
read the extant plays carefully, but he is
familiar also with the fragments of the lost
plays, with the scholia, the Alexandrian introductions, the ancient lives of the poet and
many references to him in other Greek authors.

The *Apology* is the last adventure of Balaustion, who with her husband was present in Athens when the Spartans took the city at the close of the Peloponnesian War. Aristophanes, flushed with wine and with his latest victory, meeting her and her friends, defends his art in general and his treatment of Euripides in particular. In Browning's peculiar dramatic staccato the poet leaps into our vision:

There stood in person Aristophanes.
And no ignoble presence! On the bulge
Of the clear baldness — all his head one brow —
True, the veins swelled, blue network, and there
*   surged*
A red from cheek to temple . . .

While the head, face, nay, pillared throat thrown
*   back,*
Beard whitening under like a vinous foam,
These made a glory, of such insolence —
I thought — such domineering deity
Hephaistos might have carved to cut the brine
For his gay brother's prow, imbrue that path
Which, purpling, recognized the conqueror.

This is a true picture of the poet of the *Apology* but not of the poet of the plays.

There is much spirit in the *Apology*. There
is much sorrow for fallen Athens, much insight into fifth century Greek life, substan-
tiated by compendious erudition. There is
much of the polemic and denunciatory Aristophanes, there is too much of his lewdness but
no trace of his whimsical fantasy, nor of his
clear poetry. Aristophanes cannot be recalled
to life by an elixir of elaborate allusion.
Those who do not know Aristophanes in the
original profit little by reading the *Apology*,
for they cannot understand it. Those who
know the original need not read it for the plays
are a better apology — and an easier.

Aristophanes is still, as ever, a mighty influence. He claims the attention alike of
Harriet Beecher Stowe and Bernard Shaw. To
Shaw praising the *Birds,* even as to Aristophanes, the birds seem much superior to
mortals — or to mortals' idea of God. A
recent writer in *The Yale Review* [47] hopes for
a revival of Aristophanic comedy as the only
satisfactory expression for the exasperation of
our age. George Jean Nathan wonders if
any really good comedy has been written
since Aristophanes. To Saintsbury he is the
greatest comic poet, except Shakespeare, of the

world; and Swinburne, translating the great *parabasis* from the *Birds,* calls Aristophanes: "the half divine humorist in whose incomparable genius the highest qualities of Rabelais were fused and harmonized with the supremest gifts of Shelley. . . . And my main intention, or at least my main desire," he continues, "in the undertaking of this brief adventure, was to renew as far as possible for English ears the music of this resonant and triumphant metre which goes ringing at full gallop as of horses who

> *dance as 'twere to the music*
> *Their own hoofs make.*

I would not seem over-curious in search of an apt or inapt quotation; but nothing can be fitter than a verse of Shakespeare's to praise at once and to describe the most typical verse of Aristophanes."

IX. CONCLUSION

TO his own age Aristophanes was the great writer of comedies, the caustic critic of vice public and private, the beloved poet who was rewarded for his patriotic advice to the state. To the following age he gave a standard for literary criticism, a subjective view of literature which still has vital force. To the Roman age he was at once a model for the orator and a pattern for the satirist. To the Renaissance he gave the allegorical comedy. His contribution to the modern world is not the influence which his plays have had on individual writers but it is the plays themselves — those eleven, incomparable, priceless comedies. Aristophanes is become a touchstone by which all that is keenest in wit, that is gayest in laughter, that is bitterest in ridicule and that is highest in poetry is tested. He knew in common with America's greatest humorist that "laughter is man's greatest and most neglected weapon."

For him one may paraphrase Quintilian's fine tribute to Cicero and say: "Among after generations he hath attained this, that Aristophanes is no longer the name of a man but of comedy."

NOTES AND BIBLIOGRAPHY

NOTES AND REFERENCES

1. Aristotle's *Poetics*, V, translated by S. H. Butcher, *Aristotle's Theory of Poetry and Fine Art*, London, 1920.

2. For an accurate and complete account of the Greek Theater see, R. C. Flickinger, *The Greek Theater and Its Drama*,[2] Chicago, 1922.

3. Flickinger, *op. cit.*, page 235.

4. Edward Gordon Craig, *On the Art of the Theater*, London, 1912, p. 13.

5. Cf. Mitchell Carroll, "The Athens of Aristophanes," in *Studies in Honor of B. L. Gildersleeve*, Baltimore, 1902, pp. 241–252.

6. Quoted by J. B. Bury, *History of Greece*, London, 1908, p. 457.

7. *Odyssey*, VI. 42, adapted from Butcher and Lang's translation.

8. B. L. Gildersleeve, *Hellas and Hesperia* or *The Vitality of Greek Studies in America*, New York, 1909, p. 105.

9. Thucydides, V. 28, Jowett's translation.

10. George Saintsbury, *A History of Criticism*,[3] 3 vols., New York and London, 1900–1904, Vol. I, p. 21.

11. Pliny, *Letters*, VI. 21, 5.

12. *Frogs*, 82.

13. Valerius Maximus, II. 7, ext. 7.

14. Plato, *Symposium*, XXXIX, Jowett's translation.

15. Aristotle, *Poetics*, IX, Butcher's translation.

16. Macaulay, *Essay on History*.

17. Pliny, *Letters*, VI. 21. 5.

18. *Palatine Anthology*, VII. 38; translated by W. R. Paton, *The Greek Anthology*, 5 vols., in *The Loeb Classical Library*, New York and London, 1916–1918. Cf. J. W. Mackail's *Select Epigrams from the Greek Anthology*, London and New York, 1906.

19. *Palatine Anthology*, IX. 186, Paton's translation.

20. S. H. Butcher, *Aristotle's Theory of Poetry*, p. 225.

21. Pseudo-Asconius on Cicero, *Verres, Actio prima*, 10.

22. Cicero, *De Republica*, quoted by Augustine, *De Civitate Dei*, II. 9.

23. Horace, *Satires*, II. 1. 69 and I. 10. 4.

24. Juvenal, *Satires*, I. 165.

25. Horace, *Satires*, I. 4.1. ff; G. C. Fiske in his elaborate work, *Lucilius and Horace*, Madison, 1920, discusses Horace's dependence on Lucilius and the Old Comedy.

26. Persius, *Satires*, I. 124.

27. Pseudo-Longinus, *On the Sublime*, XL. 2, Rhys Robert's translation.

28. Horace, *Satires*, I. 10. 74.

29. Quintilian, X. 1. 65.

30. Quintilian, X. 1. 100.

31. Livy, V. 21. 9.

32. Alfred et Maurice Croiset, *Histoire de la Littérature Grecque*, 5 vols., Paris, 1896–1899; and *The Works of Lucian*, translated by H. W. and F. G. Fowler, 4 vols., Oxford, 1905, Vol. I, p. XVI.

33. C. O. Zuretti, *Aristofane e Dante*, Palermo, 1901.

34. J. W. White, " The Manuscripts of Aristophanes," in *Classical Philology*, I. 1–20 (1906).

35. Matthew Arnold, *On the Modern Element in Literature*.

36. Not *the* first, cf. W. P. Mustard in *The Classical Weekly*, VI. 175 (1913).

37. Hegel, *Aesthetics*, p. 298.

38. Th. Zielinski, *Die Gliederung der Altattischen Komoedie*, Leipzig, 1885, pp. 9 seq.

39. *Ecclesiazusae*, 900 ff.

40. *Frogs*, 185.

41. Cf. B. L. Gildersleeve, in *The American Journal of Philology*, XXXIII. 227 (1912).

42. Cf. Mustard. (Note 36).

43. Walter Sichel, " The English Aristophanes," in *The Fortnightly Review*, CX (New Series). 681–704 (1911).

44. J. A. Symonds, *The Greek Poets*, II. p. 177, speaks

of the similarity between Aristophanes' *Birds* and Mozart's *Zauberflöte*.

45. Cf. D. D. Hains, "Greek Plays in America," in *The Classical Journal*, VI. 24–39 (1910–1911), and "The Presentation of Classical Plays," in *The Classical Journal*, IX. pp. 189, 251, 344 (1913–1914).

46. B. L. G., "Brief Mention," in *The American Journal of Philology*, XXXI. 487 ff. (1910).

47. John Middleton Murry, "The Break Up of The Novel," in *The Yale Review*, XII. 288–304 (see p. 303) (1923).

BIBLIOGRAPHY

BUTCHER, S. H., *Aristotle's Theory of Poetry and Fine Art*. London, 1920.

CARY, EARNEST, " The Manuscript Tradition of the Acharnenses," in *Harvard Studies in Classical Philology*, XVIII. 157–211 (1907). Also joint author with J. W. White, q. v.

CORNFORD, F. M., *The Origin of Attic Comedy*. London, 1914.

CROISET, ALFRED ET MAURICE, *Histoire de la Littérature Grecque*. 5 vols. Paris, 1896–1899.

CROISET, MAURICE, *Aristophane et les Partis à Athènes*. Paris, 1906. Translated into English by James Loeb, London, 1909.

FLICKINGER, R. C., *The Greek Theater and Its Drama*.[2] Chicago, 1922.

FRERE, J. H., *Aristophanes*, translated into English prose. London, 1874.

GELDART, W. M. (see F. W. Hall).

HAIGH, A. E., *The Tragic Drama of the Greeks*.[3] Oxford, 1907.

HALL, F. W., and GELDART, W. M., *Aristophanis Comoediae*. 2 vols. Oxonii, 1900–1907.

HILLE, CURT, *Die deutsche Komödie unter der Einwirkung des Aristophanes*. Leipzig, 1907.

HILSENBECK, FRITZ, *Aristophanes und die deutsche Literatur des 18 Jahrhunderts*. Berlin, 1908.

JACKSON, C. N., " Classical Elements in Browning's Aristophanes' Apology," in *Harvard Studies in Classical Philology*, XX. 15–73 (1909).

JEBB, R. C., *The Growth and Influence of Classical Greek Poetry*. Boston, 1894.

LEGRAND, P. E., *The New Greek Comedy*, translated by James Loeb. London and New York, 1917.

BIBLIOGRAPHY

MURRAY, GILBERT, *The Frogs of Aristophanes*, translated into English rhyming verse. London, 1912.

——, *Aristophanes and the War Party*. London, 1919.

RAPP, M., *Studien über das englische Theater*. Tübingen, 1847.

RECHNER, LEONHARD, *Aristophanes in England*. Frankfort, 1914.

ROGERS, B. B., *The Comedies of Aristophanes*. London, 1902–1916. Contains introductions to the plays, the Greek text, critical and explanatory notes and a translation into corresponding English meters. Now included in *The Loeb Classical Library*.

SETTI, GIOVANNI, " Della Fama di Aristofane presso gli Antichi," in *Rivista Di Filologia*, X. 132–182 (1882).

SHOREY, PAUL, " Aristophanes," in C. D. Warner's *Library of the World's Best Literature*. New York, 1896.

STARKIE, W. J. M., *The Acharnians of Aristophanes*. London, 1909. Contains introduction, Greek text, critical and explanatory notes and a prose translation.

——, *The Clouds of Aristophanes*. London, 1911 (similar to the above).

SÜSS, W., *Aristophanes und die Nachwelt*, in the Series, " Das Erbe der Alten." Leipzig, 1911.

SYMONDS, J. A., *Studies of the Greek Poets*.[3] 2 vols. London, 1912.

WHITE, J. W., *The Verse of Greek Comedy*. London, 1912.

——, *The Scholia on the Aves of Aristophanes*. Boston, 1914.

——, " The Manuscripts of Aristophanes," in *Classical Philology*, I. 1–20 (1906).

——, Also joint author with Earnest Cary in " Collation of the Manuscripts of Aristophanes' Aves," in *Harvard Studies in Classical Philology*, XXIX. 77 (1918), and in " Collation of the Manuscripts of Aristophanes' Vespae," in *Harvard Studies in Classical Philology*, XXX. 1 (1919).

ZIELINSKI, TH., *Die Gliederung der Altattischen Komoedie*. Leipzig, 1885.

ZURETTI, C. O., *Aristofane e Dante*. Palermo, 1901.

Our Debt to Greece and Rome

AUTHORS AND TITLES

AUTHORS AND TITLES

HOMER. *John A. Scott.*

SAPPHO. *David M. Robinson.*

EURIPIDES. *F. L. Lucas.*

ARISTOPHANES. *Louis E. Lord.*

DEMOSTHENES. *Charles D. Adams.*

THE POETICS OF ARISTOTLE. *Lane Cooper.*

GREEK RHETORIC AND LITERARY CRITICISM. *W. Rhys Roberts.*

LUCIAN. *Francis G. Allinson.*

CICERO AND HIS INFLUENCE. *John C. Rolfe.*

CATULLUS. *Karl P. Harrington.*

LUCRETIUS AND HIS INFLUENCE. *George Depue Hadzsits.*

OVID. *Edward Kennard Rand.*

HORACE. *Grant Showerman.*

VIRGIL. *John William Mackail.*

SENECA THE PHILOSOPHER. *Richard Mott Gummere.*

APULEIUS. *Elizabeth Hazelton Haight.*

MARTIAL. *Paul Nixon.*

PLATONISM. *Alfred Edward Taylor.*

ARISTOTELIANISM. *John L. Stocks.*

STOICISM. *Robert Mark Wenley.*

LANGUAGE AND PHILOLOGY. *Roland G. Kent.*

AUTHORS AND TITLES

AESCHYLUS AND SOPHOCLES. *J. T. Sheppard.*

GREEK RELIGION. *Walter Woodburn Hyde.*

SURVIVALS OF ROMAN RELIGION. *Gordon J. Laing.*

MYTHOLOGY. *Jane Ellen Harrison.*

ANCIENT BELIEFS IN THE IMMORTALITY OF THE SOUL. *Clifford H. Moore.*

STAGE ANTIQUITIES. *James Turney Allen.*

PLAUTUS AND TERENCE. *Gilbert Norwood.*

ROMAN POLITICS. *Frank Frost Abbott.*

PSYCHOLOGY, ANCIENT AND MODERN. *G. S. Brett.*

ANCIENT AND MODERN ROME. *Rodolfo Lanciani.*

WARFARE BY LAND AND SEA. *Eugene S. McCartney.*

THE GREEK FATHERS. *James Marshall Campbell.*

GREEK BIOLOGY AND MEDICINE. *Henry Osborn Taylor.*

MATHEMATICS. *David Eugene Smith.*

LOVE OF NATURE AMONG THE GREEKS AND ROMANS. *H. R. Fairclough.*

ANCIENT WRITING AND ITS INFLUENCE. *B. L. Ullman.*

GREEK ART. *Arthur Fairbanks.*

ARCHITECTURE. *Alfred M. Brooks.*

ENGINEERING. *Alexander P. Gest.*

MODERN TRAITS IN OLD GREEK LIFE. *Charles Burton Gulick.*

ROMAN PRIVATE LIFE. *Walton Brooks McDaniel.*

GREEK AND ROMAN FOLKLORE. *William Reginald Halliday.*

ANCIENT EDUCATION. *J. F. Dobson.*

ARISTOPHANES; HIS PLAYS AND HIS INFLUENCE

Aristophanes, a comic poet of great and imaginative powers, of keen wit, and remarkable lyric gifts is the major representative Athenian of Old Comedy. His plays, clever in conception and striking and successful in dramatic execution, are the works of a genius of high order.

The most riotous of Aristophanes's comedies offer penetrating criticisms on politics, education and literature. All the great satirists of Rome drew their inspiration from Aristophanes.

English drama had its origin in Greek drama which owed much to Aristophanes. The author feels that a revival of the Aristophanic comedy would prove a more satisfactory expression of the exasperation of our own age.

He discusses the comedies of Machiavelli, Rabelais, Ben Jonson and of course Gilbert (of Gilbert and Sullivan) as exemplary of the spirit of the Old Comedy.